Roots of Sorrow

BEARING THE UNBEARABLE

Bearing the Unbearable

Trauma, Gospel, and Pastoral Care

Deborah van Deusen Hunsinger

WILLIAM B. EERDMANS PUBLISHING COMPANY

GRAND RAPIDS, MICHIGAN / CAMBRIDGE, U.K.

Published 2015 by
Wm. B. Eerdmans Publishing Co.
2140 Oak Industrial Drive N.E., Grand Rapids, Michigan 49505 /
P.O. Box 163, Cambridge CB3 9PU U.K.

Printed in the United States of America

21 20 19 18 17 16 15   7 6 5 4 3 2 1

Library of Congress Cataloging-in-Publication Data

Hunsinger, Deborah van Deusen.
Bearing the unbearable: trauma, gospel, and pastoral care /
Deborah van Deusen Hunsinger.
        pages   cm
Includes bibliographical references and index.
ISBN 978-0-8028-7103-9 (pbk.: alk. paper)
1. Pastoral psychology. 2. Psychology, Religious. 3. Pastoral theology.   I. Title.

BV4012.H83   2015
253.5′2 — dc23

                                    2014049875

www.eerdmans.com

For my whole family — with deep appreciation
for their love and presence in my life

Contents

CONTENTS

Acknowledgments

Among the many important conversational partners that have contributed to my thinking over the years, I must single out my beloved husband, George Hunsinger, whose influence on my theology and my life is incalculable. His steadfast love, encouragement, and support have undergirded my vocation as a pastoral theologian and given me daily joy.

I am grateful for my years of study with a number of theological mentors at Yale Divinity School and for my treasured teacher, Ann Belford Ulanov, at Union Theological Seminary in New York City.

A number of colleagues have been important as my thought has developed, among whom Theresa F. Latini is foremost. I first met Theresa when she enrolled in the M.Div. program at Princeton Seminary in the 1990s. Many years later, after she had completed a Ph.D. in practical theology, she became my sister-in-law. Still later, she became a coauthor and coteacher as we worked together to think through the implications of contextualizing nonviolent communication for the church. I continue to be profoundly grateful for her generous, lively, and collaborative spirit.

My years of intensive study of nonviolent communication were greatly enriched by relationships developed in that community. My teachers, especially Robert Gonzales, Susan Skye, Miki and Inbal Kashtan, and Dominic Barter, contributed immensely both to my conceptual understanding and to my personal growth.

I am indebted to teachers and colleagues at the International Institute of Restorative Practices in Bethlehem, Pennsylvania, and to the STAR program (Strategies for Trauma Awareness and Resilience) at Eastern Mennonite University in Harrisonburg, Virginia. Mark Vander Vennen of

FaithCare in Toronto was a faithful companion and guide as I learned how to bring restorative practices to the church.

I am also indebted to the generous sabbatical leaves granted by the trustees of Princeton Theological Seminary, which enabled me to craft each of the chapters in this volume with care.

I am also grateful to Vinod Gnanaraj for the preparation of the index.

To all my friends and colleagues — spiritual direction groups and prayer groups, students and former students, counselees and supervisees — I owe profound debts of gratitude for the many ways in which we have shared our lives as I have struggled with the complex ideas developed in this book.

Above all, the love of my family — not only that of my parents, Robert Holt and Martha Moon van Deusen, but also that of my brothers and sisters, my husband, children, and grandchildren — has formed the essential matrix in which my mind and heart have been shaped. Grateful to be so richly blessed, I dedicate this book to them.

I am grateful for permission to reprint material that first appeared in earlier publications:

"Bearing the Unbearable: Trauma, Gospel and Pastoral Care," *Theology Today* 68, no. 1 (2011): 8-25.

"Forgiving Abusive Parents," in *Forgiveness and Truth,* ed. Alistair McFadyen and Marcel Sarot (New York: T&T Clark, 2001), 71-98. Reprinted by permission of Bloomsbury Publishing Plc.

"Keeping an Open Heart in Troubled Times: Self-Empathy as a Christian Spiritual Practice," in *A Spiritual Life: Perspectives from Poets, Prophets, and Preachers,* ed. Allan H. Cole (Louisville: Westminster John Knox, 2011), 123-34.

"Prayers of Lament," in *Pray without Ceasing* (Grand Rapids: Eerdmans, 2006), 138-55.

"Practicing Koinonia," *Theology Today* 66, no. 3 (October 2009): 346-67.

"Members of One Another: Building a Restorative Church," in *Theology in Service to the Church,* ed. Allan H. Cole (Eugene, Ore.: Wipf and Stock, Cascade Books, 2014), 155-79. Used by permission of Wipf and Stock Publishers. www.wipfandstock.com.

Introduction

I envision trauma as a series of nested concentric circles, affecting every level of our lives, beginning with the suffering involved in facing our own mortality and personal capacity for evil and reaching progressively outward to traumas that have greater scope: with the next circle comprising the interpersonal traumas of divorce, death, disease, or disability affecting ourselves or those we love. As the concentric circles grow larger, we encounter the kind of trauma that has the betrayal of trust at its core: infidelity, domestic violence, rape, incest, and child abuse.

Intergenerational trauma that is often passed from one generation to the next includes the indelible impact of assault, suicide, or murder on families and communities. Moving further out toward a wider scope and greater impact, we find that the next concentric circle entails the crushing structural violence of poverty, homelessness, imprisonment, racism, enslavement, immigration, and political oppression. Finally, in the outermost circle of hell, we encounter not only the terror of natural and ecological disasters but also the moral catastrophes of war, torture, genocide, and terrorism.

Pastoral theology, as a contemporary field of inquiry, has long studied those issues in the middle circles, shedding light on the complex suffering that comes in the wake of disease, death, violence, and abuse, focusing especially on its interpersonal, familial, and community impact. The rise of psychology in the twentieth century, joined now by breakthroughs in neuroscientific research, has given pastoral theology deeper insight into the multiple causes of trauma as well as suggested multiple approaches to its healing.

In recent decades, the field of pastoral theology has shifted from exclusively clinical or therapeutic considerations (regarding both diagnosis and treatment) to wider cultural, economic, and political considerations, addressing in one way or another virtually every form of human suffering mentioned. Like every discipline in theological study, pastoral theology is intrinsically interdisciplinary, as it builds bridges of scholarly conversation with a wide number of fields: not only psychology and psychotherapy in relation to theology and biblical studies, but also economics, sociology, political science, ethics, literary studies, poetry and the arts, criminal justice, and peace studies.

This volume reflects some of those shifts, examining trauma from a number of interpretive frameworks that are then brought into dialogue with Christian theology. While psychology and psychotherapy continue to be primary conversation partners, other disciplines contribute to the discussion, particularly those that have developed the theoretical underpinnings and practical strategies for restorative practices (primarily social work, criminal justice, and education). The overriding aim of the book is to illuminate the impact of trauma on people's lives and to present conceptual frameworks and practical strategies for healing, particularly in a North American context, from a center in the gospel. Each chapter weaves together various theoretical and practical threads with the faith, practice, and theology of the church. For if the scope of trauma's impact is envisioned as a series of nested concentric circles, so also the gospel's restorative power is understood to emanate outward, as the presence and work of Jesus Christ mercifully address every kind of human misery and need.

Christ's healing and reconciling work, completed once for all in his death on the cross, continues to radiate outward, reaching persons and communities, and even nations that are reeling from overwhelming pain at every level of their common life. By Word and sacrament, through preaching and prayer, and through those who hunger and thirst for justice both within and outside the church, Christ's work is attested and mediated to the world. By God's mercy, it reaches the minds and hearts of those afflicted with trauma. Those who are far from remembering the goodness of God, who carry personal memories of horror in their bodies and souls, receive the ministry of compassionate witnesses willing to share their burden of suffering. By God's grace, many of the afflicted find pathways to wrest wisdom from a tangle of pain. Because trauma is not a single event but a complex series of events, what happens after a traumatic episode may be as significant as the episode itself. This is the point at which enduring post-traumatic distress might even be prevented. It is at this juncture that human sufferers most need their fellow human beings to demonstrate care for them, to hear their story, however fragmented or inchoate, with compassion. For finally, human beings are able to bear the unbearable only as others are willing to bear it with them.

Yet, because God alone can bear the full weight of sin and death — the manifold ways that human beings hurt, maim, and destroy each other with their words, deeds, and deadly weapons — those in the church learn to rely not on the strength of their own meager efforts, but on the One who reveals the vast reaches of God's compassion, Jesus Christ. They recognize that it is only through God's grace, mercy, and loving compassion that both survivors and witnesses are able to keep their equanimity when hopelessness threatens. As the community bears one another's burdens through compassionate witnessing, it relies not so much on its own skill and resourcefulness as on its trust in the redemptive suffering of Christ.

Chapter 1, "Bearing the Unbearable: Trauma, Gospel, and Pastoral Care," traces the recent history of trauma studies, describes trauma's symptoms, and offers guidance in those "best practices" that promise healing. It then offers theological reflection for understanding trauma in the light of Christian faith. The chapter is written to serve as a basic primer for pastors and lay caregivers as they seek to offer sensitive, compassionate care to those suffering from trauma.

Chapter 2, "Rooted and Grounded in Love: Compassionate Witnessing," draws on the generative work of family therapist and clinical psychologist Kaethe Weingarten as it considers what it means to become an active and empowered witness of the suffering of others. After setting forth several of Weingarten's key ideas, I endeavor to place them within a Christian theological context.

Chapter 3, "Christian Forgiveness: Healing the Emotional Wounds of Childhood," considers the traumatic impact of abusive parenting on children, by drawing on depth psychological findings and family systems research. These perspectives are then brought into conversation with Christian theology, which serves essentially to reframe them. A psychological understanding of healing is contrasted with and ordered in relation to a theological understanding of forgiveness. If the different logical levels of these concepts (psychological and theological) are not respected, confusion is the result. Theological reflection offers a unique understanding of the spiritual challenges faced by those who suffer from early childhood abuse, while Christian faith offers a unique perspective on post-traumatic growth.

Chapter 4, "Keeping an Open Heart in Troubled Times: Self-Empathy as a Christian Spiritual Practice," examines the plight of the pastoral caregiver (or compassionate witness) faced with compassion fatigue or vicarious traumatic stress. How can empathic and caring persons continue to listen to the anguished stories of others without becoming overwhelmed themselves? A practical strategy is introduced, by means of nonviolent communication's teachings on the practice of self-empathy, with its countercultural understanding of human needs. Christian theology reinforces the perception that ultimately God alone can open one's heart, granting caregivers the gift of *willingness* to share in the painful mourning of others.

Chapter 5, "Prayers of Lament: 'How Long, O Lord?'" describes an ancient Christian practice that enables the afflicted to keep hope alive. Only by keeping the channel of communication and communion with God open is a person able to stay alive spiritually. Without an impassioned cry of lament directed toward God, believers can be cast adrift in a chaotic sea of pain and despair. Lament paradoxically deepens the sufferer's connection to God despite all signs of God's absence. It gives strength to endure even in the shadow of death.

Chapter 6, "Practicing *Koinonia:* Life Together," begins with a theological description of God's gift of *koinonia* (communion, fellowship, partnership) to the church. Whenever "brothers and sisters dwell together in unity," this gift becomes visible as a living parable of God's kingdom here on earth. The skills offered by nonviolent communication are described and placed in service to this telos, as empathic listening, speaking honestly, and self-empathy are presented as practical tools for dealing with criticism, avoiding pastoral burnout and pastoral misconduct, and deepening our life of prayer. Skills of empathy are placed into a christological framework to show how they can be used faithfully in our witness to a compassionate God.

Chapter 7, "Members of One Another: Building a Restorative Church," introduces a set of practices that seems to be little known in the church, although it is widely used elsewhere to help communities in distress. Here the focus is on congregational trauma, as I seek to glean what is useful from the transdisciplinary field of restorative practices. Transdisciplinary studies combine the knowledge of a number of academic fields with the hands-on knowledge and skill of nonacademic practitioners. In this case, criminal justice, education, counseling, social work, organizational management, and theology each responds creatively not only to the fragmentation of knowledge in academic disciplines but also to the growing interpersonal disconnection in our communities. The chapter offers a practical model for working with churches in distress while showing the model's congruence with basic themes of the gospel, particularly the interdependence of all members of the community and the ultimate aim of reconciliation for all parties, not only victims of harm but also those who have perpetrated it, as well as those members of the community vitally affected as witnesses. Some form of justice needs to be extended to all those affected, not only the victims and families of those directly harmed but also everyone in the surrounding community, for "if one person suffers, all suffer together."

The book closes with two brief appendices for easy reference, one summarizing the symptoms of trauma as delineated in the Diagnostic and Statistical Manual (DSM-5), and the other a metric developed to help caregivers determine their level of potential burnout or compassion fatigue, called the "Compassion Satisfaction and Fatigue Subscales."

The book seeks to provide conceptual resources for the upbuilding of the church of Jesus Christ as an exercise in pastoral theology. Near the end of his life the apostle Paul wrote that though he was afflicted in every way, he was not crushed; though perplexed, he was not driven to despair; though persecuted, he was not forsaken; and though struck down, he was not destroyed (2 Cor. 4). By the mercy of God, he did "not lose heart."

What enabled one so afflicted to keep his heart open toward the misery of others, to know God's mercy so intimately that he could extend that mercy even toward those who sought to destroy him? What enabled him not to lose heart in the midst of ongoing persecution and suffering? Paul reminds his readers that though the church has its treasure in earthen vessels, it nevertheless does have a treasure. It is the treasure given to those who have eyes to see "the light of the gospel of the glory of Christ, who is the likeness of God" (2 Cor. 4:4).[1] Paul sees the vast scope of God's grace extending always further outward, to reach peoples everywhere: "As grace extends to more and more people it may increase thanksgiving, to the glory of God. So we do not lose heart" (2 Cor. 4:15-16). May this work serve God's glory by helping its readers not to lose heart in these challenging times.

---

1. Unless otherwise indicated, all Scripture quotations in this book come from the Revised Standard Version.

CHAPTER 1

Bearing the Unbearable

Trauma, Gospel, and Pastoral Care

Traumatic loss lies at the very heart of the Christian imagination. The souls of those who call themselves Christian are indelibly stamped with the unbearable sorrow of this man, Jesus. After raising the hopes of many, Jesus died a shameful death, indeed an unjust and horrible death. What is more, his friends denied, betrayed, and abandoned him in his hour of need. He was tortured and executed as a common criminal, even though he had done nothing to warrant condemnation. Jesus Christ drank the cup of bitterness all the way to its dregs, and descended into the very depths of hell: How can such a terrible story be borne? Much more than an intellectual puzzle about so-called theories of atonement is at stake here. Believers who have survived trauma stake their very lives on the power of the gospel to heal.

Trauma: How can we give it the kind of disciplined attention that it deserves? Holding even a fraction of this suffering steadily in our attention can be challenging. Is it possible to talk about trauma without causing pain to those already bearing trauma in their bodies and souls?[1] Daily through the media, we are bombarded with stories capable of breaking our hearts, yet little attention is given to the impact of such accounts on their hearers. How can we bear these stories with an open heart?[2] Indeed, how do we bear them at all?

---

1. Serene Jones asks a similar question: "How can ministers craft sermons that speak to the plight of trauma survivors without retraumatizing them?" See Serene Jones, *Trauma and Grace: Theology in a Ruptured World* (Louisville: Westminster John Knox, 2009), 85.

2. See chapter 4 in this volume, "Keeping an Open Heart in Troubled Times: Self-Empathy as a Christian Spiritual Practice."

Pastoral theology, as I understand it, is first and foremost a theology of *God's care* for the world in Jesus Christ, in which we are invited to participate.[3] This means that all pastoral care depends upon prayer, leads to worship, and trusts in the promises of God. Such an orientation leads us to confess that though we ourselves, with our enduring failures to love, cannot truly redeem traumatic loss, we cling in hope to the One who can and does. That One drank the cup of bitterness, died a death of anguish, and descends into every darkness that threatens to overwhelm us.

Those who study theology are called to ponder holocausts of every kind, from biblical "texts of terror,"[4] to grueling historical or theological tracts, to the horrors of the evening news. How can we fortify ourselves, our students, or our children for the kind of world we live in? Whether painted on a vast canvas of national or international significance, or in a miniature of a single family or community, traumatic loss is ubiquitous. When it hits us personally, it changes our lives irrevocably: through the shock of an accident, a criminal assault, or a tragic death, or through the multiple and complex traumas that arise in relation to immigration, war, imprisonment, torture, domestic violence, or sexual abuse, among others. Unacknowledged and unhealed, trauma often leads to further violence, either against oneself or against others, and thus to more trauma. With knowledgeable intervention and wise support, however, trauma can be healed, and may even become "a catalyst for growth and transformation,"[5] the turning point of a life, a sign and symbol of God's goodness and care.

As caregivers in the church who seek to help others, how can we be sure that we will *first do no harm?* How can we be a source of spiritual strength and practical support for the communities we serve? Moreover, as witnesses to the trauma of others or as persons afflicted by trauma ourselves, where do we turn for help? In this chapter, I want to set forth an understanding of the impact of trauma and inquire into the role of the gospel and the church in its healing. I plan to address three basic issues:

- What is trauma and how does it affect us?
- How do we break free from the vicious cycle of trauma's impact?

3. See Andrew Purves, *Reconstructing Pastoral Theology: A Christological Foundation* (Louisville: Westminster John Knox, 2004).

4. Phyllis Trible, *Texts of Terror: Literary-Feminist Readings of Biblical Narratives* (Philadelphia: Fortress, 1984).

5. Patricia Mathes Cane, *Trauma Healing and Transformation: Awakening a New Heart with Body-Mind-Spirit Practices* (Watsonville, Calif.: Capacitar, 2000), 17.

- How does the gospel with the pastoral care of the church bring healing to the traumatized?

What Is Trauma and How Does It Affect Us?

The twentieth century offered countless opportunities for studying trauma, but it was not until the 1970s that social and political ferment enabled its study to advance decisively.[6] By the mid-1970s, hundreds of "rap" groups had been organized by Vietnam Veterans against the War where men could speak honestly about the horror of war. At the same time, women gained collective courage as they shared, among other things, their stories of rape, sexual abuse, or domestic violence. No longer willing to allow "denial, secrecy and shame"[7] to render them mute, both men and women were able to transform what had previously been private suffering into powerful public action for social and political change. In the 1970s and 1980s, crisis centers, rape hotlines, and safe shelters were established with painstaking effort in state after state.[8]

At the same time, the Veterans Administration commissioned thorough studies of the war's impact on returning Vietnam vets.[9] Subsequently, a "five-volume study on the legacies of Vietnam . . . demonstrated beyond any reasonable doubt [the] direct relationship [of trauma] to combat exposure."[10] With multiple vectors for social change converging, the American Psychiatric Association included a new diagnosis in its Diagnostic and Statistical Manual for 1980 called post-traumatic stress disorder (PTSD). In their first attempt to capture its essence, psychiatrists described trau-

6. For a fascinating account of the history of the study of psychological trauma, see Judith Herman's classic text, *Trauma and Recovery* (New York: Basic Books, 1997), chap. 1.

7. Herman, *Trauma and Recovery*, 29.

8. For the fascinating and distressing article "History of Battered Women's Movement," see www.icadvinc.org/what-is-domestic-violence/history-of-battered-womens -movement/, accessed December 16, 2014. The following quotations cite Del Martin, *Battered Wives* (New York: Pocket Books, 1976), 4. "A study in Chicago reveals that from September 1965 to March 1966, 46.1% of the major crimes perpetrated against women took place in the home. It also found that police response to domestic disturbance calls exceeded total response for murder, rape, aggravated assault, and other service crimes." "From 1968 to 1973, the crime of rape increased 62% nationwide." With a statistic like this, one wonders whether the crime actually increased so dramatically or whether the increase was due to more and more women being willing to acknowledge and report it.

9. Herman, *Trauma and Recovery*, 27.

10. Herman, *Trauma and Recovery*, 27.

matic events as lying "outside the range of usual human experience,"[11] a definition that proved untenable since traumatic incidents of one kind or another are quite common.[12] As psychiatrist Judith Herman writes: "Traumatic events are extraordinary, not because they occur rarely, but rather because they overwhelm the ordinary human adaptations to life."[13] In fact, a simple thumbnail definition of trauma might be: "an inescapably stressful event that overwhelms people's coping mechanisms."[14] When people face "intense fear, helplessness, loss of control, and the threat of annihilation,"[15] and when these feelings persist for more than a month, PTSD becomes the chosen diagnosis.[16] Witnesses to horrific events are also vulnerable to trauma. Watching helplessly as a loved one dies, seeing the Twin Towers fall to the earth, or listening in fear as one's mother or sibling gets beaten — such events can trigger a traumatic reaction.[17]

The subjective experience of feeling overwhelmed uniquely characterizes trauma and differentiates it from those situations that are experienced, perhaps, as exceptionally stressful but not as traumatic. Peter Levine elaborates: "Traumatized people . . . are unable to overcome the anxiety of

11. Herman, *Trauma and Recovery*, 33.

12. "Norris (1992), in a study of 1,000 adults in the southern United States, found that 69% of the sample had experienced a traumatic stressor in their lives, and that this included 21% in the past year alone." From Bessel A. van der Kolk, Alexander C. McFarlane, and Lars Weisaeth, eds., *Traumatic Stress: The Effects of Overwhelming Experience on Mind, Body, and Society* (New York: Guilford Press, 2006), 135.

13. Herman, *Trauma and Recovery*, 33.

14. Van der Kolk, McFarlane, and Weisaeth, *Traumatic Stress,* 279.

15. N. C. Andreasen, "Posttraumatic Stress Disorder," in *Comprehensive Textbook of Psychiatry,* ed. H. I. Kaplan and B. J. Sadock, 4th ed. (Baltimore: Williams and Wilkins, 1985), 918-24, quoted in Herman, *Trauma and Recovery,* 33.

16. Following the criteria for diagnoses can be dizzying since PTSD has so many close cousins, such as acute stress disorder, panic disorder, anxiety disorder, agoraphobia, etc. However, a synopsis of the seven criteria of PTSD are: (1) the traumatic stressor involves death, injury, or serious threat (or witnessing or learning about such occurring to another); (2) the response involves intense fear, helplessness, or horror; (3) the person persistently reexperiences the traumatic event; (4) the person persistently avoids stimuli associated with the trauma and tries to numb general responsiveness; (5) symptoms of hyperarousal persist; (6) they persist for a month or more; (7) and the symptoms cause "clinically significant distress or impairment in social, occupational, or other important areas of functioning." See appendix 1.

17. See Kaethe Weingarten, *Common Shock: Witnessing Violence Everyday* (New York: New American Library, 2003). See also Kaethe Weingarten, "Witnessing the Effects of Political Violence in Families: Mechanisms of Intergenerational Transmission and Clinical Interventions," *Journal of Marital and Family Therapy* 30, no. 1 (January 2004): 45-59.

their experience. They remain overwhelmed by the event, defeated and terrified. Virtually imprisoned by their fear, they are unable to re-engage in life. Others who experience similar events may have no enduring symptoms at all. . . . No matter how frightening an event may seem, not everyone who experiences it will be traumatized."[18] The imponderable factor here is that the nature of the triggering event in and of itself does not guarantee a traumatic reaction.[19] One person may experience the event as traumatic while her neighbor, friend, or daughter experiencing the exact same event may find it stressful, but not traumatic. This fact remains completely inexplicable until we realize that *none of us ever actually has the exact same experience* because our minds organize our experiences in a completely idiosyncratic way. The meaning of an experience will be different for each person because our way of making narrative sense of our lives is utterly unique. Thus, feeling overwhelmed or immobilized is a variable that cannot be predicted by either the nature, magnitude, or intensity of the triggering event.[20] *"Consequently,"* writes Carolyn Yoder, *"a traumatic reaction needs to be treated as valid, regardless of how the event that induced it appears to anyone else."*[21]

I believe this point is fundamental to competent pastoral care. Time and again one hears people minimizing or discounting the anguish of others, essentially encouraging them to "get over it." Wanting those they love to be whole, they try to encourage them by *rationally explaining* why they should not be upset by so small a thing. Yet, nothing so completely obstructs the healing process as having someone offer the free advice to "get over it" or "put it behind" them. While such defense mechanisms — denial and minimization — on the part of friends or caregivers are understandable human reactions to pain in those they love, they only injure the traumatized further, perhaps to the point of shaming them into silence and truly unbearable isolation.

Yet, why *aren't* they able simply to "get over it"? The various symptoms of post-traumatic stress have been aptly summarized by Judith Herman as *hyperarousal, intrusion,* and *constriction:* *"Hyperarousal* reflects the per-

18. Peter Levine, *Waking the Tiger: Healing Trauma* (Berkeley: North Atlantic Books, 1997), 28.

19. For a thoughtful analysis of the most salient etiological factors that specify a likelihood of vulnerability to PTSD, see Alexander C. McFarlane and Rachel Yehuda, "Resilience, Vulnerability, and the Course of Posttraumatic Reactions," chapter 8 in van der Kolk, McFarlane, and Weisaeth, *Traumatic Stress,* 155-81.

20. Carolyn Yoder, *The Little Book of Trauma Healing* (Intercourse, Pa.: Good Books, 2005), 10.

21. Yoder, *The Little Book,* 11.

sistent expectation of danger; *intrusion* reflects the indelible imprint of the traumatic moment; *constriction* reflects the numbing response of surrender."[22] While each symptom originates in the triggering event itself, they all have an afterlife in the person's unfolding post-trauma history.

Any kind of physical or emotional shock has the potential to set certain physiological responses in motion. Typical responses include an increased pulse rate, difficulty in breathing, rising blood pressure, and constriction of the stomach. One's thoughts may begin to race and the skin may become cold. These responses all stem from the autonomic nervous system putting the body on high alert in response to a perception of threat. The release of hormones mobilizes the body for fight or flight. When neither fight nor flight seems possible, the physiological response of the body is to freeze.[23]

In the freeze response, "the victim of trauma enters an altered reality. Time slows down and there is no fear or pain. In this state, if harm or death do occur, the pain is not felt as intensely."[24] There is a notable shift in consciousness, in which there is a subjective sense of detachment. Victims of sexual assault, for instance, sometimes speak of "leaving their body" and watching themselves from another point in the room: standing next to the bed or looking down from the ceiling.[25] Metaphorically, it is as if the soul escapes the body to protect the person from the physical pain and the full emotional impact of his radical vulnerability.

Like the *fight or flight* response, *freezing* is heralded by a flood of hormones. In 1844, Dr. David Livingstone described his subjective experience of being seized by a lion: "Growling horribly close to my ear, he shook me as a terrier dog does a rat. It produced a sort of dreaminess in which there was no sense of pain, nor feeling of terror, though I was quite conscious of all that was happening. . . . This placidity is probably produced in all animals killed by the carnivore; and if so, is a merciful provision of the Creator for lessening the pain of death."[26] The capacity of the mind to dissociate like this may reduce the immediate pain and horror of the event, but it does so at a high cost. Studies now demonstrate that "people who enter a dissociative state at the time of the traumatic event are among those most likely to develop long-lasting PTSD."[27]

22. Herman, *Trauma and Recovery*, 35.

23. Babette Rothschild, *The Body Remembers: The Psychophysiology of Trauma and Trauma Treatment* (New York: Norton, 2000), 8.

24. Rothschild, *The Body Remembers*, 10.

25. Herman, *Trauma and Recovery*, 43.

26. www.heroesofhistory.com/page13.html, accessed December 16, 2014.

27. Herman, *Trauma and Recovery*, 239.

During a traumatic ordeal, the intense hyperarousal of the emotions often "interfere[s] with proper information processing and the storage of information in narrative (explicit) memory."[28] This means that memory of the trauma is often fragmented; it is not organized in a linear, narrative fashion as normal memories are. Instead, certain features associated with sensory data are vividly remembered such as a particular smell, sound, image, or color. If a dog was barking when the person was assaulted, for instance, the sound of a barking dog might evoke subsequent feelings of terror or rage, yet strangely unaccompanied by an explicit memory of the assault. Or, alternatively, the memory of the assault may be explicit, yet strangely dissociated from the accompanying emotions. Bessel van der Kolk comments:

> Although the individual may be unable to produce a coherent narrative of the incident, there may be no interference with implicit memory; the person may "know" the emotional valence of a stimulus and be aware of associated perceptions, without being able to articulate the reasons for feeling or behaving in a particular way. [Pierre] Janet [1859-1947] proposed that traumatic memories are split off (dissociated) from consciousness, and instead are stored as sensory perceptions, obsessional ruminations or behavioral reenactments.[29]

Such intrusive memories can be quite distressing, as aspects of the traumatic event are replayed in the mind over and over again, but without the full picture, without the experience of "normal memory" that enables a coherent sense of self-understanding.

After such an event, the hyperarousal of the nervous system keeps persons on a kind of "permanent alert,"[30] where they may startle easily and sleep poorly. Subject to nightmares and intrusive flashbacks, they may begin to circumscribe their world to avoid anything that might retrigger the feelings of helplessness, rage, fear, grief, panic, and shame associated with the event. Flashbacks are something like having nightmares while awake. Something triggers the memory of the trauma, perhaps the smell of alcohol, the sound of a particular footfall, a certain tone of voice or characteristic gesture. Indeed, anything can trigger a flashback because of the way the brain organizes data in a vast web of interconnected associations.

28. Van der Kolk, McFarlane, and Weisaeth, *Traumatic Stress,* 286.
29. Van der Kolk, McFarlane, and Weisaeth, *Traumatic Stress,* 287.
30. Herman, *Trauma and Recovery,* 35.

Neurologists remind us that neurons that "fire together, wire together."[31] Two or more things are forever associated, "wired together" in the brain's neural pathways. Suddenly, one is shaking and sweating in response to an ordinary, everyday event.[32] Yet, knowing that one's response is out of proportion to what triggered it only increases a sense of powerlessness, anxiety, and shame. Because such experiences of intrusion are so frightening and because survivors can make little rational sense of them, survivors often do whatever they can to avoid these states or to deaden the pain by numbing out in some way.

If they do not actively seek help, a whole range of defensive patterns may develop. Rather than facing the pain directly, survivors may turn the intense traumatic energy against themselves. Many addictive behaviors have their source in unresolved trauma that is not consciously faced: substance abuse, workaholism, eating disorders, even rituals of self-mutilation can seem preferable to experiencing the buried pain of trauma.[33] Shame, dread, and helplessness are pervasive, alternating with numbness, depression, or a sense of emptiness. Their sense of agency is damaged; they often feel powerless and alone in a hostile world, wondering whether anyone cares if they live or die.[34] Spiritual questions may become particularly intense with a growing sense of disorientation or even meaninglessness. Living in an unsafe world, survivors of trauma put themselves on constant alert, watching for danger.

While many victims suffer in silence, others turn the intensity of their suffering outward. Feelings of rage may predominate. They want justice, and fantasies of revenge may become an obsession. Sometimes narratives are created where the plotline of good versus evil has them perpetually in the role of the "good guy," with "the other" as the "bad guy." The enemy

31. See Daniel Siegel, *The Developing Mind: How Relationships and the Brain Interact to Shape Who We Are* (New York: Guilford Press), chap. 4.

32. "Painful life experiences get encoded in our brains and bodies and can be reactivated with great intensity by the right kind of trigger decades later, even if we believe that we have dealt with them or have completely forgotten about them." A. J. van den Blink, "Trauma and Spirituality," in *Reflective Practice: Formation and Supervision in Ministry*, vol. 28 (Decatur, Ga.: Journal of Pastoral Care Publications, 2008), 30-47, here 38.

33. Yoder, *The Little Book*, 33.

34. Feeling helpless and alone in a potentially hostile world was Karen Horney's definition of neurosis. See *Neurosis and Human Growth: The Struggle toward Self-Realization* (New York: Norton, 1950). Serene Jones speaks repeatedly throughout her book of the damaged sense of agency of the traumatized and their need for experiences of empowerment. See *Trauma and Grace.*

is typically seen as less than fully human. The traumatized begin to tell a predictable tale that seldom varies. Pastoral theologian David Augsburger challenges victims of trauma with a number of pointed questions: "Can I identify what I get out of rehearsing an offense over and over? Why do I insist on replaying the history of injury? How often have I told and retold the story of the offense to others to gain their support and validation of my role or position as victim?"[35] When such desires for revenge are not consciously wrestled with, attacks on others may seem justified as a way of restoring a sense of dignity, respect, and honor, or in the name of justice.[36] In a chilling comment, James Gilligan, director of the Center for the Study of Violence at the Harvard Medical School, comments that "All violence is an effort to do justice or to undo injustice."[37] Pain that is not transformed does not simply disappear. As Ann Ulanov writes:

> Where we repress our grudge-holding, our wish to make someone pay for what has happened to us . . . that repressed shadow does not just go away. It goes unconscious and remains alive with instinctual impulses, emotions, but far out of reach of modification by social or personal reality testing. . . . We put onto others what we do not own in ourselves and identify them with this rejected bit of ourselves. The personal becomes social. But then this live bit of shadow menaces us from the outside.[38]

Instead of the trauma being "acted in" against the self, it is now "acted out" against others. The traumatized feel justified in venting their rage, yet such repeated venting only serves to inscribe the anger and sense of moral outrage more deeply in body and soul. It does nothing to bring healing or peace.

Freud describes "repetition compulsion" as a symbolic reliving of the trauma, as a way the traumatized express their suffering while yet failing to become fully conscious of it. Children who have been sexually abused, for example, may engage in ritual play that gives unconscious voice to the

---

35. David Augsburger, *Hate-Work: Working through the Pain and Pleasures of Hate* (Louisville: Westminster John Knox, 2004), 227.

36. Howard Zehr, "Doing Justice, Healing Trauma: The Role of Restorative Justice in Peacebuilding," *South Asian Journal of Peacebuilding* 1, no. 1 (Spring 2008): 15.

37. James Gilligan, *Violence: Reflections on a National Epidemic* (New York: Random House, 1996), quoted in Zehr, "Doing Justice, Healing Trauma," 5.

38. Ann Belford Ulanov, *The Unshuttered Heart: Opening to Aliveness/Deadness in the Self* (Nashville: Abingdon, 2007), 140-41.

abuse. Those honored for bravery in war may suffer repetitive nightmares[39] or else wreak terrible violence on their families[40] as they struggle with mental pain. The combination of survivor guilt, depression, frozen grief, anguish, and rage acts as a kind of seething cauldron beneath the surface, ready to burst forth in a symbolic reenactment of the original horror, often with tragic results.

How Do We Break Free from the Vicious Cycle of Trauma's Impact?

Is it possible to forge a path that seeks neither "oblivion" on the one hand nor "revenge" on the other?[41] Is it possible truly to heal? Ann Ulanov describes the predicament of those who have constricted their lives in the aftermath of trauma.

> We swap aliveness for restriction in order to feel safer, avoid pain, survive some blow that seems to us unbearable, that would destroy us. We fear we are empty inside so we cover it up with manufactured control, or made-up excitement, or self-promotion. The emptiness can never change if we refuse to experience it, and in the company of an other. We need an other to depend on when we turn to face our deadness. Whatever we are afraid of, it requires our attention; we must go down into it, look around, not knowing if and how we will come out.[42]

Three key phrases need to be underlined here: First, whatever the traumatized are afraid of *requires their attention.* Second, they need to experience it *in the company of an other.* And third, they take these steps *not knowing if and how they will come out.*

Those who seek to reclaim their lives after trauma need to face what

---

39. Harry Wilmer, "The Healing Nightmare: A Study of the War Dreams of Vietnam Combat Veterans," *Quadrant* 19, no. 1 (Spring 1986).

40. See the story told by "Gizelle" in which the unhealed suffering of war leads to sexual assault with horrific effects in Ellen Bass and Laura Davis, *The Courage to Heal: A Guide for Women Survivors of Child Sexual Abuse,* 4th ed. (New York: Harper and Row, 2008).

41. Bessel van der Kolk dedicates his remarkable anthology, *Traumatic Stress: The Effects of Overwhelming Experience on Mind, Body, and Society,* "to Nelson Mandela and all who, after having been hurt, work on transforming the trauma of others rather than seeking oblivion or revenge."

42. Ulanov, *The Unshuttered Heart,* 38.

has actually happened to them. *It requires their attention.* If their nervous system is in a hyperaroused state, they need to find as much safety as possible. Only true safety will provide the emotional security needed to begin the healing process commonly known as mourning. Giving voice to all they have experienced — the terror and helplessness, the sense of moral outrage and personal violation, the sorrow, hurt, anger, and grief — becomes the essential first step in piecing together a coherent narrative.

Yet none of this can happen apart from the lively presence of *a caring other.* Who can bear the anguish of such a narrative, without minimizing or denying it, without giving advice or offering strategies to overcome it? Who can listen without offering empty platitudes or switching the focus to a similar story of his own? Who has the wisdom to refrain from asking intrusive questions prompted by his own anxiety, allowing the traumatized person space to tell his story in his own way at his own pace? Who can offer a compassionate, caring presence, free of pity or sympathy, free of judgment, praise, or blame?[43]

Healing begins as the traumatized begin to piece together a coherent narrative, creating a web of meaning around unspeakable events while remaining fully connected emotionally both to themselves and to their listener. It takes courage even to begin such a conversation. Their feelings can be confusing and difficult to sort out. Often there seem to be no words that adequately describe the horror. Moreover, is it safe to trust the listener? Feelings of shame, fear of judgment, extreme vulnerability are common. Maybe talking about it will make matters worse.

Talking about it can, in actual fact, make matters worse. Any kind of direct processing of the traumatic experience needs to be balanced at all times with a sense of safety and containment. Anchoring oneself in the present, feeling safe with one's listener, processing one small piece at a time, mourning each of the profound losses involved — all these steps take time, patience, and exquisite self-care. Trauma specialists are trained to pay attention to signs of distress and deliberately slow down the process, remembering the maxim that "the slower you go, the faster you get there."[44] The goal in talking about it is to stay fully connected to the feelings without

---

43. Training in *nonviolent* or *compassionate communication* teaches an exquisite awareness and concrete strategies for the kind of empathic attunement described here. See Marshall Rosenberg, *Nonviolent Communication: A Language of Life* (Encinitas, Calif.: PuddleDancer Press, 2003).

44. Jon G. Allen, *Coping with Trauma: Hope through Understanding,* 2nd ed. (Washington, D.C.: American Psychiatric Publishing, 2005), 251-53.

becoming overwhelmed. Eye contact with the caregiver, slowing down the pace, taking a break from the past, returning to the present with clear focus on one's bodily sensations — all help to put on the brakes.[45] Understanding what is happening and why profoundly assists the healing process as well. This is why a clear conceptual understanding of trauma is important: understanding becomes a part of the holding environment that contains anxiety and increases a sense of empowerment.[46]

Those who have courageously faced trauma give powerful witness to the risks involved. Will they choose life by facing the pain, or will they shrink back once again into numbing defenses?

> When I get into a crisis now, instead of saying, "Oh my God, I'm never going to heal," I see that it's like layers, and the more I work with it, the more they keep coming around. And even though it's like "But I was feeling good two days ago and now I'm shaking and crying and I can't sleep," I'm beginning to see that I'm not coming back to the same place. I'm coming back at a different level. . . . When I reach the next level where the tears are, where the fear is, where the tiredness is, I have to trust.[47]
>
> For me the decision not to identify with the past was a decision, not just a change I went through in the healing process. I had to make a quantum leap that I was no longer going to have the abuse be the cause and my life be the effect. . . . Right now you have to choose what standpoint you are going to live life from. And it's a constant choice.[48]

Trauma survivors need to choose life over death, not once but many times, reaching out with the fragile hope that the trauma can be healed or transformed, that the pain will abate, or that some kind of normalcy will re-

45. Babette Rothschild writes: "I never help clients call forth traumatic memories unless I and my clients are confident that the flow of their anxiety, emotion, memories, and body sensations can be contained at will. I never teach a client to hit the accelerator, in other words, before I know that he can find the brake." See http://www.saskworld.com/bodymindspirit/edition21/17_article_rothschild.htm, accessed July 10, 2010.

46. "Developing a cognitive frame that helps patients understand their intrusions and avoidance helps them gain some emotional distance from the experience, and begins to put the event into the larger context of their lives." See Bessel van der Kolk, Alexander C. McFarlane, and Onno van der Hart, "A General Approach to Treatment," in van der Kolk, McFarlane, and Weisaeth, *Traumatic Stress*, 426.

47. Bass and Davis, *The Courage to Heal*, 457.

48. Bass and Davis, *The Courage to Heal*, 438.

turn. Some try to take their lives. Tragically, many succeed, despairing that nothing can stop the eternal recurrence of the trauma. Each person needs the love, support, respect, and understanding of caring others.[49] Those who grow through and beyond trauma do so in part by forging a spiritual framework for what is called post-traumatic growth. Not knowing if or how they will come out, they nevertheless are freed to take steps toward greater and greater freedom. It is to one such framework that I now turn.

How Does the Gospel with the Pastoral Care of the Church Bring Healing to the Traumatized?

When we enter "the strange new world of the Bible," we are confronted with paradox and mystery at every turn. Here we behold a crucified Savior, a God who bears our grief and carries our sorrow, who heals by taking away the sin of the world, both the evil we suffer and the evil we do. It makes no rational sense. Looked at from outside the circle of faith, it is a complete conundrum. "Getting in" on this religion wrenches your mind inside out: Is the cross of Christ sheer foolishness or is it the very power of God (1 Cor. 1:18)?

At its core, the cross becomes gospel for the traumatized only if they are able to see there a *divine love* willing to bear what is unbearable for mortal, fallen human beings. God bears for us the full weight of both sin and death. If God in Jesus Christ descends into the worst hell imaginable in order to deliver us from the hells we inflict upon one another, then such a God is worthy of our trust. We need not stand by helplessly witnessing the suffering and dying of those we love; we have a God to whom we can entrust them in life and in death. For Jesus Christ is not simply a human companion who comforts us by suffering trauma alongside us. As the creeds of the church attest, he is known to us as the risen Lord, the very Wisdom and Power of God, through whom God will fulfill his purpose of redemption. Jesus Christ, the gospel attests, bears what cannot be borne by fragile, fallen human beings. He alone bears the sin of the world, and he alone bears it away.

As the Lamb of God who *takes away* the sin of the world, Christ is known as that One who suffers *for* our sake as well. On our behalf and for

---

49. Sometimes teens and children are overlooked. Where early attachment is threatened or ruptured, children are much more vulnerable to trauma throughout their lives. See the valuable work done by the National Child Traumatic Stress Network for helpful resources. http://www.nctsnet.org. I am indebted to Jennie Olbrych for this reference.

our sake, he takes human depravity into his own divine heart in order to transform it, so that it no longer has the power to separate us from God. The powers of sin and death that have such a hold on us — *and that are at the root of all trauma* — are finally nullified. Not only the fear of death, by which human beings are made "subject to lifelong bondage" (Heb. 2:15), but also the fear of eternal estrangement from the very Source of Life, is proclaimed to be overcome in Christ. Through Christ, we have access to all that we long for: the loving gaze of one who cherishes us, miraculous outpourings of grace, a steady anchor in times of distress, mercy on our weakness, forgiveness of our sins, and most basic of all, the lifeline of basic trust.

If salvation means forgiveness of sin and the promise of eternal life, then all our pastoral arts of healing have *this promise* as their telos. Healing, whether physical, emotional, or spiritual, is always set within this larger context of the unimaginable reaches of God's salvation.[50] If our hope is nothing less than the salvation *of the world* in Jesus Christ, it is also a hope held out for the *perpetrators* of trauma as well as for its *victims*. All those human beings from whom we normally seek to separate ourselves by every conceivable means, those perpetrators of unspeakable horror — they, too, perhaps more than anyone, need to hear the gospel word of God's judgment and mercy. If One died for all, then he died for those who have brought the terrors of hell, not only upon others, but also upon themselves through their own actions.[51]

Indeed, whenever we affirm that Christ died for sinners, we affirm our solidarity with all who do harm, solidarity in sin as well as in our deliverance from sin. In confessing ourselves as sinners, utterly unable to save ourselves, we recognize that under similar circumstances of deprivation, terror, or colossal historic evils, we, too, would be capable of monstrous

---

50. See Deborah van Deusen Hunsinger, *Theology and Pastoral Counseling: A New Interdisciplinary Approach* (Grand Rapids: Eerdmans, 1995). See also Robert W. Jenson, "Story and Promise in Pastoral Care," *Pastoral Psychology* 26, no. 7 (1977): 113-23. "In historical fact and by manifest anthropological necessity, nothing but final hope ever sustains genuine suffering or enables creative historic action."

51. "More recently has come an awareness of 'perpetrator-induced trauma' and its role in perpetuating the cycle of victimization and offending; severe offending can itself cause trauma in offenders." Zehr, "Doing Justice, Healing Trauma," 10. See also Robert MacNair, *Perpetration-Induced Traumatic Stress: The Psychological Consequences of Killing* (Westport, Conn.: Praeger, 2002). For a compelling story, see Wendell Berry, "Pray without Ceasing," in *Fidelity* (New York: Pantheon Books, 1992), 3-60.

crimes toward our fellow human beings. The cross of Jesus Christ is God's response not only to the terror of human trauma but also to the anguish of human guilt, bringing succor and healing to the one, and judgment, forgiveness, and the "godly grief" of repentance to the other (2 Cor. 7:10). When we affirm the resurrection and ascension of Jesus Christ, we affirm his power to bring every kind of evil to an end. "Though innocent, Christ suffers as if guilty and ends the logic of evil by taking our suffering onto his body, and not being destroyed by it nor by the death it inflicts. The abyss of love is revealed as stronger than the abyss of death, the power of love as stronger than the power of hate."[52] This is an interpretive framework that no psychiatrist or therapist has to offer, no twelve-step program or self-help group can claim, but which can be preached and taught week after week in the context of ordinary pastoral care: that in overcoming the world, Jesus Christ saves us from both the guilt and anguish of human sin, as well as the terror and trauma of suffering and death.

These are words of hope to which the traumatized may cling. "Now hope that is seen is not hope" (Rom. 8:24). Though our faith holds us fast to this hope, we know that many descend into their graves with nothing but hatred toward those who have harmed them or those they love. Forgiveness, though freely given by God, does not seem to be a human possibility for us in turn. Try as we might, it does not seem subject to our human will but comes, when it does, as a miracle of God.[53] While not *subject* to our human will, forgiveness rarely happens apart from an active decision to forgive. Pastoral theologian David Augsburger gives one definition of forgiveness: it "is an act of laying aside one's rational arguments for repayment, my principled arguments for my being truly in the right and you being wholly in the wrong, and at last offering a full and complete pardon to the other, whether or not there are any believable signs of authentic remorse or repentance in the perpetrator. In granting the other person release, one receives one's own."[54] We have seen this miracle of forgiveness in the testimonies of those who appeared before the South African Truth and Reconciliation Commission. One that has stayed with me is the testimony of Ms. Babalwa Mhlauli. Bishop Tutu writes, "When she had finished telling her story, she said she wanted to know who had

---

52. Ulanov, *The Unshuttered Heart*, 150-51.

53. Deborah van Deusen Hunsinger, "Forgiving Abusive Parents," in *Forgiveness and Truth*, ed. Alistair McFadyen and Marcel Sarot (New York: T. & T. Clark, 2001), 71-98.

54. Augsburger, *Hate-Work*, 232.

killed her father. She spoke quietly and, for someone so young, with much maturity and dignity. You could have heard a pin drop in that hushed City Hall when she said, 'We do want to forgive but we don't know whom to forgive.' "[55] We see it in Marietta Jaeger-Lane, who has worked tirelessly for both victims *and* perpetrators in the years that followed the kidnapping and murder of her seven-year-old daughter, Susie. Founder of Murdered Victims' Families for Reconciliation, Ms. Jaeger-Lane continues to honor her daughter by offering testimony to end capital punishment for capital crimes.[56] Such stories challenge us to consider those for whom we harbor ill will, those we are unable or unwilling to forgive. Sometimes, we can only lay them at the foot of the cross for God to judge, confessing our inability to fathom either the extent of the evil or its redemption. We can only point away from ourselves to the transcendent hope of the gospel we are called to proclaim.

If maintaining hope is the foundation of all healing, as psychotherapist Jon G. Allen attests, then the gospel has something fundamental to offer those afflicted by trauma.[57] While ministry cannot replace the work of psychiatry or psychotherapy, it can nevertheless function as an indispensable part of the healing process.[58] When human trust has eluded them, the traumatized desperately need an anchor, a point of reference, something or someone reliable in which to place their trust. Scripture attests again and again that by the power of the Spirit, God comes to those who cry out for help:

55. Desmond Tutu, *No Future without Forgiveness* (New York: Doubleday, 1999), 149.

56. Testimony of Marietta Jaeger-Lane on behalf of Murder Victims' Families for Human Rights and Journey of Hope, an act abolishing the death penalty and replacing it with life imprisonment without possibility of release, Senate Judiciary Committee Hearing, February 7, 2007. http://4and20blackbirds.wordpress.com/2009/03/24/bill-to-abolish-death-penalty-hearing-is-wednesday/, accessed December 16, 2014. "To say the death of any other person would be just retribution is to insult the immeasurable worth of our loved ones who are victims. We can not put a price on their lives. In my case, my own daughter was such a gift of joy and sweetness and beauty, that to kill someone in her name would have been to violate and profane the goodness of her life; the idea is offensive and repulsive to me." See also Marietta Jaeger, *The Lost Child* (Grand Rapids: Zondervan, 1983).

57. Allen, *Coping with Trauma*.

58. In the United States context, those diagnosed with PTSD will often turn for help to therapists especially trained in trauma. In other contexts around the world, imaginative rituals and collective healing processes have been developed. See, for example, the work of Martha Cabrera, "Living and Surviving in a Multiply Wounded Country," describing her work in Nicaragua. www.envio.org.ni/articulo/1629, accessed November 14, 2014.

I called on Your name, O Lord,
From the lowest pit.
You have heard my voice:
"Do not hide Your ear
From my sighing, from my cry for help."
You drew near on the day I called on You,
And said, "Do not fear!"   (Lam. 3:55-57 NKJV)

We thus facilitate healing when we help the afflicted cry out their sorrow, rage, and tears *to God*. Prayers of lament — crying out to God for deliverance — seem to be faith's only alternative to despair.[59] Instead of protecting themselves against the pain, the afflicted are encouraged to go down into it, clinging to God's promises as they do so. Listen to one such lament, in which the afflicted one directs her anguish toward God.

There comes a time when both body and soul
enter into such a vast darkness
that one loses light and consciousness
and knows nothing more of God's intimacy.
At such a time, when the light in the lantern burns out
the beauty of the lantern can no longer be seen,
with longing and distress we are reminded of our nothingness.
At such a time I pray to God:
"O God, this burden is too heavy for me!"
And God replies:
"I will take this burden first and clasp it close to Myself
and that way you may more easily bear it." . . .
If God leaves me unanointed, I could never recover.
Even if all the hills flowed with healing oils,
and all the waters contained healing powers,
and all the flowers and all the trees dripped with healing ointments,
still, I could never recover.
"God, I will tear the heart of my soul in two
and you must lie therein.
You must lay yourself in the wounds of my soul."[60]

59. Deborah van Deusen Hunsinger, "Prayers of Lament," in Hunsinger, *Pray without Ceasing: Revitalizing Pastoral Care* (Grand Rapids: Eerdmans, 2006).
60. Marchiene Vroon Rienstra, *Swallow's Nest: A Feminine Reading of the Psalms*

These words of Mechthild of Magdeburg, a mystic of the thirteenth century, echo down through the centuries, offering a startling image of healing through the palpable presence of Christ's own body. In her fervent prayer, Mechthild offers the wounds of her soul for healing through the intimate presence of Christ's broken body. Here we meet profound mystery. An image of union with Christ rises up from the depths and is given voice in her prayer. Only the full, living presence of a wounded Savior can heal her soul.

Psychologist Robert Stolorow speaks of the fundamental necessity of finding what he calls a "relational home" for traumatic experience. He writes, "Trauma is constituted in an intersubjective context in which severe emotional pain cannot find a relational home in which it can be held. In such a context, painful affect states become unendurable."[61] Severe emotional pain cannot be endured if it does not have a relational home, someone to hold what cannot be borne.[62] Ministers of the gospel of Jesus Christ who are rooted and grounded in the love of God provide just such a relational home for all those who groan for the redemption of the world. They offer a steady, sturdy, compassionate, and loving witness to all who have suffered trauma. Insofar as they thus participate in Christ's own compassion, they become witnesses to and mediators of Christ's miraculous grace.

Conclusion

In recent decades pastoral theology has turned more and more to the public, social, and political dimensions of both affliction and pastoral care. Ministers of the church not only attend to individual members of their congregations but also participate in larger communities of outreach and care. Especially in the light of recent large-scale disasters, pastoral leaders need to respond with sensitivity to the needs of those who do not share the gospel narrative as the overarching context of meaning of their lives. I

(Grand Rapids: Eerdmans, 1992), appendix. From *The Flowing Light of the Godhead*, by Mechthild of Magdeburg, Cistercian nun (1210–ca. 1285).

61. Robert D. Stolorow, *Trauma and Human Existence: Autobiographical, Psychoanalytic, and Philosophical Reflections* (New York: Routledge, 2007), 10.

62. See also the example in chapter 4 below. The experience described there illustrates the importance of having one's pain "witnessed" as described by Weingarten in *Common Shock*.

believe that it is crucial for us also to address questions such as these, even though they lie outside the scope of this chapter.[63]

As leaders in their own church communities, pastors need to recognize the power inherent in their position to frame and interpret any traumatic event that has occurred. In so doing, they can either inflame the situation by escalating anxiety (through name-calling, rushing to judgment and blame, using us/them dichotomies, labeling dissenting views, or withholding or misrepresenting the facts)[64] or decrease anxiety and facilitate healing by opening channels of communication among all parties involved.[65] As they offer a secure holding environment to strengthen frayed bonds of trust, and as they call upon God to minister to the community in its pain, they offer space to the hurting to tell their story. In some cases, nearly everyone in the community has been hurt by trauma, but in strangely diverse ways.[66] In this kind of situation, it is essential that pastors

---

63. Jeannette Sutton writes about the wariness that disaster coordinators have toward providers of spiritual care who volunteer their assistance. "There has been unease about hidden agendas, the appropriateness of religiously oriented interventions, and concern for victims who might feel that contact with some minister-types is intrusive and assaultive." "Convergence of the Faithful: Spiritual Care Response to Disaster and Mass Casualty Events," *Journal of Pastoral Theology* 16, no. 1 (Fall 2006): 19. Through ministries of "presence" and "hospitality," spiritual care providers in the public sphere offer comfort and reassurance while helping victims to draw upon their "own religious and/or spiritual resources in order to construct meaning out of chaos." They respect personal boundaries, know how to work in an interfaith manner, and are responsive to training from the disaster assistance professionals such as the American Red Cross.

64. Vamik Volkan, *Blind Trust: Large Groups and Their Leaders in Times of Crisis and Terror* (Charlottesville, Va.: Pitchstone Publishing, 2004), cited in STAR training, "Part III: The Trauma Healing Journey, Breaking the Cycles of Violence," Eastern Mennonite University, 2002.

65. See Howard Zehr, *The Little Book of Restorative Justice* (Intercourse, Pa.: Good Books, 2002), 67-69.

66. Ministers themselves are vulnerable to any trauma afflicting their community. Pastors and church leaders occupy a unique dual role, as those called to give pastoral care, yet at the same time as human beings who are themselves personally affected. Those in caregiving roles need to be exquisitely attuned to their own needs for care, especially when their immediate community is in crisis. Ministers' families are vitally affected and need support as well. Presbyterian Disaster Assistance (PDA) consists of PCUSA pastors, elders, and mental health professionals who are trained in trauma and crisis response, who offer companionship and support to church leaders in congregations affected by "human-caused disasters." I am indebted to Katherine Wiebe, who serves on the PDA, for this point. Dr. Wiebe founded the Institute for Congregational Trauma and Growth for congregations experiencing disaster, violence, or trauma. See www.ictg.org.

refrain from moralizing or blaming, but position themselves in such a way that all persons can be heard.[67] The community needs to gather in order to share their common grief, which serves to counteract the fear, shame, isolation, and horror of what has occurred.[68]

The pastoral care of the community finds its final locus in ritual, psalm, and song, in worship and the mystery of the Lord's Supper. Personal trauma and loss are woven into the losses of the larger community as the liturgy unfolds. That which is most deeply personal becomes part of the communal lament of the people of God through the ages. Walter Brueggemann reminds us that the "public dimension of grief is deep underneath personal loss, and for the most part, not easily articulated among us. But grief will not be worked well or adequately until attention goes underneath the personal to the public and communal. My expectation is that pastors, liturgically and pastorally, most need to provide opportunity and script for lament and complaint and grief for a long time. No second maneuver after grief shall be permitted to crowd in upon this raw, elemental requirement."[69] By permitting an unrelieved descent into the raw emotions of grief within the secure boundaries of ritual space, hope and trust may be paradoxically restored.[70]

As the church gathers for worship, we are told of a God who is "the Father of mercies and God of all comfort, who comforts us in all our affliction, so that we may be able to comfort those who are in any affliction, with the comfort with which we ourselves are comforted by God" (2 Cor. 1:3-4). In worship we find space both to mourn and to hope, as we wait with painful longing for the redemption of the world. We find comfort in the midst of affliction when we are reminded that the One who descends into every human hell we create, and unwittingly or maliciously perpetuate, is the very One who sits at the right hand of the Father in glory.

The community that responds to trauma in these ways will, by the grace and power of God, find itself stronger, wiser, more compassionate, and more resilient. Its collective story will be one of overcoming adversity

67. Zehr, *The Little Book,* 67-69.

68. Zehr, *The Little Book,* 19-41.

69. Walter Brueggemann, as cited by John Swinton, *Raging with Compassion: Pastoral Responses to the Problem of Evil* (Grand Rapids: Eerdmans, 2007), 121.

70. See Cedric C. Johnson, "Unspeakable Things Spoken: Globalization, Imperial Trauma and the Development of African American Identities" (Ph.D. diss., Princeton Theological Seminary, May 2010), for a description and analysis of a whole community engaged in a transformative healing process as they confront horrific historic and ongoing trauma.

together rather than a story of shame, revictimization, fear, and silencing. By reclaiming the essential practices of our faith — compassionate witnessing, communal lament, and public worship — we "enable people to continue to love God in the face of evil and suffering and in so doing to prevent tragic suffering from becoming evil."[71] As John Swinton writes, "Loving God does not take away the pain that [trauma] inflicts, but it *does* transform it."[72] May God work out our salvation by bearing what cannot be borne, by transforming our mourning into longing, our longing into lament, our lament into hope, and, through the redemption of this beloved world, our hope into joy.[73]

71. Swinton, *Raging with Compassion*, 85.

72. Swinton, *Raging with Compassion*, 75.

73. I am indebted to colleagues George Hunsinger, Katherine Sonderegger, Katherine Wiebe, and Barbara Chaapel for valuable comments on earlier drafts of this chapter.

CHAPTER 2

Rooted and Grounded in Love

Compassionate Witnessing

Trauma depends upon the conviction that what we are faced with cannot be borne. We feel overwhelmed and helpless, not knowing how to deal with trauma's treacherous symptoms. Sometimes we either lack awareness of the possibility of support or desire to protect others from our pain. The lack of support — or the belief that, for a variety of reasons, we cannot secure it — helps unlock the mystery of why some are more prone to post-traumatic stress than others. It is not so much the intensity of the stressor that determines whether we are traumatized, in other words, as it is the presence (or absence) of others who are willing to show their care for us when we are overwhelmed.

Some events are obviously so horrific that anyone would become overwhelmed. Events such as slavery, torture, captivity, and war come readily to mind. In the aftermath of catastrophe, violence, or violation, we need what Kaethe Weingarten has called a "compassionate witness."[1] While much of the trauma literature focuses on those who are either victims of violence or perpetrators of violence, a third category of people is often overlooked. It includes all who witness violence or violation. It is the role of the witness that Weingarten leads us to consider.[2] In this chapter we will examine Weingarten's key concepts in order to deepen our under-

---

1. See Kaethe Weingarten, *Common Shock: Witnessing Violence Every Day* (New York: New American Library, 2003).

2. Shelly Rambo's fascinating book *Spirit and Trauma: A Theology of Remaining* (Louisville: Westminster John Knox, 2010) considers the role of the witness in a more strictly theological sense. With the traumatic story of Jesus' death and descent into hell as her focus, Rambo sounds many familiar themes, particularly the challenge of speaking and writing on a topic "given the profound shattering of language and meaning in trauma." Instead of "comprehension and understanding," our rhetoric needs to shift to one of "witnessing and testifying" (27-28).

standing of trauma's scope. Not all stressful incidents lead to PTSD, yet one cannot predict in advance what will — or will not — lead to traumatic symptoms. Weingarten reminds us that all of us witness violence and violation every day. Typically we respond to such occasions with what she calls "common shock." Some of these "shocks" induce traumatic symptoms in the witness while others do not. Weingarten offers a theoretical framework through which such situations can be analyzed. She wants to help witnesses become both aware and empowered so that they can be helpful to those more directly affected. In this chapter, we will seek to understand the role of the witness in situations of traumatic stress. We will then offer some reflections on Weingarten's work from a Christian perspective.

In the course of an ordinary day we might witness a mother bark orders at her child in the grocery store, read about people killed in an accident, hear a story of rape, and talk with a friend diagnosed with a terminal illness. As we witness the suffering of others — some more distant and some closer to home — we become vulnerable to its emotional impact. Common shock is the emotional impact of violence or violation on the witness. The shocks we undergo may or may not have a traumatic impact on us, but as the examples show, they are common and ordinary, a part of everyday life.

As the instances of suffering and pain edge closer to home, witnesses stand in danger of becoming overwhelmed, just as the victims and perpetrators are, because to be placed in the presence of trauma is to witness horror secondhand.[3] It is to enter a realm that many would choose to avoid. While the task for the sufferer is to resist isolation, the task for the witness is to refuse indifference.[4] Instead of fleeing, compassionate witnesses choose to stay present. Weingarten, recognizing the difficulty of the task, offers a variety of conceptual resources, inspiring stories, and clinical observations for engaging the suffering of others.

How do we develop the skills we need to witness another's suffering? In her book *Common Shock: Witnessing Violence Every Day,* Weingarten addresses the question in detail. A clinical psychologist, family therapist, and professor at Harvard Medical School, Dr. Weingarten seeks to empower those who witness violence to become conscious witnesses rather

---

3. See Robert MacNair, *Perpetration-Induced Traumatic Stress: The Psychological Consequences of Killing* (Westport, Conn.: Praeger, 2002), cited in Howard Zehr, "Doing Justice, Healing Trauma: The Role of Restorative Justice in Peacebuilding," *Peace Prints: South Asian Journal of Peacebuilding* 1, no. 1 (Spring 2008): 10.

4. Kaethe Weingarten, "Hope in a Time of Global Despair," http://www.witnessing project.org/our-projects, accessed January 10, 2014.

than reactive or numb bystanders. She chooses the term "common shock" rather than "trauma" because she believes that not all response to violence or violation warrants a mental health diagnosis. Common shock is just that: common to all humanity. It belongs to being human. Shock might lead to an acute or chronic stress reaction, to trauma symptoms, or to full-blown post-traumatic stress disorder. The phrase "common shock," in other words, is meant to cover a wide range of responses that have varied consequences for the individual, her interpersonal relationships, her community, the larger society, and the world. Common shock comes to nations, to communities, to families, and to individuals through a variety of means: a medical diagnosis, a chronic disability, a criminal assault, a tornado, a flood, a bombing, or a politically oppressive regime, among others. While some people might undergo an acute stress reaction and others might need therapeutic help for post-traumatic stress disorder, many who undergo severe stress do not need or even seek medical attention. The difference between a shocking event that leads to trauma and one that does not, Weingarten suggests, might lie more in the individual's or community's response to the event than in the event itself. Thus the decisive question becomes: Are there witnesses available who are willing to listen compassionately to those devastated?

Weingarten draws on her own life experience to elucidate some of the sufferer's dilemmas. At one point she describes the painful isolation she experienced after a year of cancer treatments. "My life was bleak and lonely because I lived in silence: certain that no one could bear to hear the feelings and thoughts I had following my year of treatment; unwilling to find out if I was right; certain that I needed to protect people from my experience; and failing in those few times that I tried to put into words the chaos of my emotions and the terror that lived in my flesh."[5] As she worked through her personal impasse, Weingarten came to see that a person's ability to give voice to his suffering is not the achievement of the lone individual, but depends instead upon "the willingness of the listeners that make up the person's community. In this view, voice is contingent on who listens with what attention and attunement. Voice depends on witnessing."[6] Weingarten's life took a dramatic turn once she broke free from her self-imposed isolation, when she began to question the assumption that she needed to protect those she loved from her fear and despair.

5. Weingarten, "Witnessing, Wonder and Hope," *Family Process* 39, no. 4 (Winter 2000): 390.

6. Weingarten, "Witnessing, Wonder and Hope," 392.

Though compassionate witnessing does not remove the pain of trauma, it reconfigures it by restoring human connection, building strength and hope even in the midst of tragedy. According to Weingarten, three key elements are involved: selecting a witnessing focus; listening with care and responding with compassion; and undertaking a concrete action that addresses the other's need, either literally or symbolically.[7] In order not to be overwhelmed by grief or paralyzed into inaction, the witness must actively choose a witnessing focus that is doable. Selecting a focus is a creative process that requires the witness to connect one's "understanding of a situation with one's response to it and bring this into alignment with one's resources, commitments and values."[8]

When a beloved violin repair store burned to the ground, Weingarten was concerned about how it would affect her four-year-old son. Ben admired the violins and had come to know the store owners through periodic visits to the store with his mother. Believing that knowledge of the fire would be devastating for him, Weingarten diverted their route home for several days. On their regular day for making bread, they walked past the place where the store had been reduced to ashes. Ben's mother made sure to give her son time to express his shock at the burned building and his distress over the lost violins. After a time, she asked him what he would want the store owners to know. Ben replied, "I'm sorry that the violins burned." She then asked whether he'd like to shape a loaf of bread into a violin and give it to the store owners as a way of saying they were sorry about their loss. Ben thought that was a fine idea. Making the dough, kneading it, shaping it, and baking it gave the mother and son time to reflect together on the loss and its meaning. They took the bread, still warm from the oven, to the store's owners. With his mother's help, the shy lad lifted up the cookie sheet with the bread violin, as an expression of their care. The owners were moved by their kind gesture. And Ben, very early in life, learned that in situations of loss and distress, it is possible to do something that effectively offers comfort to others.[9]

The story illustrates each of Weingarten's key points. She wanted to choose a focus that would enable her son to feel his feelings, to express them in a safe and reflective space, and then to do something constructive with his response. The overall process was designed to undercut the sense of helplessness that often emerges in the wake of tragedy, en-

---

7. Weingarten, *Common Shock,* 192-93.
8. Weingarten, *Common Shock,* 193.
9. Weingarten, *Common Shock,* 193-94.

abling Ben to experience his own action making a difference. All three elements that are essential to compassionate witnessing are here: selecting a workable focus, offering compassionate presence, and taking empowering action. The creativity of Weingarten's strategy becomes clear as each of the particulars is examined. Weingarten's son was four. The repair store was especially beloved. The mother and son had a weekly bread-baking ritual already in place, an activity that enabled reflective time together. What is more, Weingarten had given herself a few days to process her own feelings about the fire before letting her son know about it. This choice enabled her to be a calm presence for Ben as he worked through his feelings. Her question to Ben reveals that she had already selected a specific witnessing focus: "What do you want the store owners to know?" she asked. She had selected a focus that she trusted would be meaningful to Ben, who already had a relationship with the store owners.

With more complex issues, in incidents involving groups of people rather than a single individual, and in events that are more shocking to the witness as well as to the one being witnessed, the witnessing focus and the symbolic action chosen would have to be adjusted.

Moving from the familial to the professional sphere, and from a simple common shock to more complex matters, Weingarten argues that it is crucial for particular professionals to become skilled at compassionate witnessing, especially those who experience what she calls "double jeopardy." Educators, health-care professionals, police, clergy, and journalists, she says, "expose themselves daily, repetitively, and cumulatively to the violence and violation that permeates the lives of their constituents."[10] It is imperative that those who function in these roles develop habits of mind and heart that enable them to be both aware and empowered so that they will, "first, do no harm." Though fundamental to the Hippocratic oath taken by those in the medical profession, the vow not to do harm implicitly pervades professional training in every field. Indeed, it is hard to imagine anything more disheartening than to discover that one has actually done harm rather than the good one intends.

Weingarten differentiates four possible "witness positions" and encourages her readers to identify situations in their own lives in which they can see themselves in each of these four quadrants.[11]

10. Weingarten, *Common Shock,* 93.
11. Weingarten, *Common Shock,* 95.

	AWARE	UNAWARE
EMPOWERED	1	2
	Effective, competent	*Misguided, possible malpractice*
DISEMPOWERED	4	3
	Ineffectual, stressed	*Abandoning, possible malpractice*

The ideal position for the witness is to be both aware and empowered, a position illustrated by the story of making the bread violin in response to the shock of seeing the destroyed store. Weingarten could place herself in witness position 1, both *aware* of the significance the burned store might have for her son and *empowered* as she witnessed his shock, helped him process his feelings, and undertook a symbolic action of care with him. What is more, she taught her son how to stay aware and empowered himself as he witnessed the loss.

Those who are professionally trained to help, teach, heal, protect, and report the suffering of others seek to place themselves in this witness position *(aware and empowered).*[12] Here they experience themselves as effective in what they are called to do. They have an awareness of the suffering of those they serve as well as a sense of empowerment in relation to that suffering. Imagine a nurse who thrives in her work. She knows both her responsibilities and her limits; she cares about her patients and their needs, and has a vast array of resources ready at hand. Gifts of healing, well-honed skills, practical wisdom, and a commitment to serve are combined in a way that helps others through some of the most stressful days of their lives: time spent as a patient in a hospital. Though the nurse witnesses suffering daily, she has enough resiliency and resources (both personal and structural) to get up the next day and serve again with an open heart.

By contrast, witness position 2 — *empowered but unaware* — is the most dangerous of the witness positions, for here the witness has power over others but little or no awareness of the significance of what she is witnessing. Weingarten discusses the terrible legacy of clergy sexual abuse of children, in which the Catholic hierarchy failed to develop procedures by which perpetrators would be held accountable for their actions. Not only did no one intervene to protect the children in the first place, but church officials who learned of the abuse after the fact sought to cover it up by transferring offenders elsewhere. Though the church had abundant

12. Weingarten's discussion of witness positions can be found in chapter 5 of *Common Shock.*

resources regarding the process of repentance and making amends, it made little apparent use of them. Victims, families, churches, and the society as a whole suffered because those in positions of power failed to act on behalf of those most vulnerable in their care. Situations of malpractice are likely to occur whenever people have power over others but have no clear structures of accountability and little awareness of the violence they are perpetuating.

Witnesses in position 3, *unaware and disempowered,* are unaware and therefore disempowered in relation to the violence they are surrounded by. Teachers who lack internalized models of care from mentors and who also lack training in compassionate witnessing might close their eyes to the structural violence of their institutional setting and so perpetuate it for another generation. According to one study cited by Weingarten, "Students hear anti-gay slurs approximately 25 times a day," but faculty "intervene in fewer than 3 percent of occurrences."[13] The students' sense of hopelessness skyrocketed when teachers were present but said or did nothing to stop the slurs. Their failure to take action magnified the students' sense of powerlessness. Whenever there is widespread failure to address an issue, it is likely a symptom of the whole system's failure or even an entire culture's blind spot. It is possible that some teachers, aware of the violence but lacking knowledge of how effectively to intervene, endeavored to stay unaware of the problem by ignoring it.

Witness position 4, *aware and disempowered,* is the position most likely to lead to empathic stress reactions. When those who witness violence are aware of the harm being done but feel disempowered to help, they become vulnerable to ongoing distress. Professionals in this witnessing position suffer from various syndromes: burnout, empathic distress, secondary (or vicarious) traumatic stress, or compassion fatigue. Each syndrome entails a cluster of symptoms suffered by those who are aware of the significance of what they are witnessing but are disempowered, either through a lack

13. M. Bochenek et al., *Hatred in the Hallways: Violence and Discrimination against Lesbian, Gay, Bisexual, and Transgender Students in U.S. Schools* (New York: Human Rights Watch, 2001), cited in Weingarten, *Common Shock,* 97. Given the sea change that has occurred in cultural attitudes toward LGBT people over the course of the past decade, one would hope that these statistics would be drastically different today. See "Building a Restorative Practice Curriculum in Middle and High Schools in the U.S.," by Gerald Monk, Ph.D., at http://www.iirp.edu/pdf/Hull-2010/Hull-2010-Monk.pdf, for a creative approach that addresses complex cultural attitudes and trains school personnel in practical strategies to bring about cultural shifts. Accessed July 2014.

of personal skill or by the structural violence of their institutional setting. "Empathic stress reactions," says Weingarten, "are a severe form of common shock that persists over time."[14] The symptoms of burnout can be physical, emotional, relational, or spiritual. Perhaps all four dimensions will be present. Witnesses might suffer from migraines, ulcers, heart palpitations, panic attacks, general malaise, lack of energy, perplexing fits of anger, or growing cynicism. They might question their sense of calling, blame themselves for their lack of effectiveness, or even fall into a depressive state. Feelings of self-doubt and shame may intensify, causing them to withdraw from those in whom they usually confide, which contributes to a sense of isolation and increases the likelihood of a continuing downward spiral. "Secondary traumatic stress," another form of empathic stress, can also emerge in witness position 4. It "refers to the effects . . . of being exposed to another person's trauma . . . [and] is usually accompanied by intense feelings of horror, helplessness and fear."[15] Unlike burnout, which can creep up on people slowly, secondary or vicarious traumatic stress can happen suddenly when people witness something that triggers feelings of horror.

"Compassion fatigue," a term coined by psychologist Charles Figley, refers to the exhaustion and dysfunction that come with ongoing exposure to one who is suffering.[16] Caregivers of family members who are chronically ill would be familiar with the symptoms of compassion fatigue, as would ministers or chaplains who regularly accompany those who are seriously ill or dying. Therapists who witness trauma on a daily basis are at risk both for secondary traumatic stress (experiencing the trauma of another through ongoing witnessing of it) and for compassion fatigue (reaching the limit of their resources for compassion in the presence of so much suffering).

These four witnessing positions give implicit acknowledgment to the risks involved in seeing suffering on an ongoing basis and refusing to be indifferent or make oneself numb to the needs of others. Compassionate witnesses allow themselves to feel the impact of another's pain; they recognize the common humanity of all who suffer, what Buddhist monk Thich Nhat Hanh describes as our essential "interbeing." "My well-being, my happiness, depends very much on you, and your well-being, your happiness, depends on me. I am responsible for you and you are responsible for me. . . . Therefore in order to take care of you, I have to take care of

---

14. Weingarten, *Common Shock,* 100.
15. Weingarten, *Common Shock,* 100.
16. Weingarten, *Common Shock,* 81.

myself."[17] Because compassionate witnesses understand human interdependence, they strive to pay as close attention to their own needs as they do to the needs of others. One hospital chaplain I know chose to work only four days a week. She had negotiated her work schedule to work four-fifths time with Thursdays off, so that she could stay home and sleep through the entire day. Knowing how deeply restorative sleep was for her, she sought a strategy that enabled her to function effectively as a hospital chaplain for more than twenty-five years. Weingarten comments on all those who regularly witness the pain of others, demonstrating the importance of witnessing the witnesses.

> The symptoms of secondary traumatic stress are similar to the symptoms of posttraumatic stress disorder and they remit to similar interventions. People can suffer from either of these empathic stress reactions or a combination of both. These responses are normal, common, expectable, and still, often not recognized. Or they are recognized, but the person feels considerable shame about them. Sadly, these occupational hazards of witnessing violence and violation are interpreted by many people — both within and outside of these professions — as signs of personal failure.[18]

Clearly they are not signs of personal failure. On the contrary, they are signs of a conscious choice to bear the burdens of others. They betray faith and courage, not shame and failure.[19]

Weingarten's personal history makes her particularly alert to forms of common shock experienced in witnessing the suffering of others. Throughout her writings, she offers her own self-witness, giving her readers the opportunity to learn from her varied experiences. When her mother was dying of cancer, Weingarten learned that her father wanted the family to withhold from her mother the truth of her diagnosis so that she would not "lose hope."

---

17. Weingarten, *Common Shock*, 223.
18. Weingarten, *Common Shock*, 105.
19. See "Professional Quality of Life Scale: Compassion Satisfaction and Fatigue Subscales," in appendix 2, developed by B. Hudnall Stamm, a questionnaire designed to help people assess their vulnerability to burnout and compassion fatigue or secondary trauma, as well as determine the level of satisfaction they derive from being in a profession that calls upon their capacity to respond compassionately to others. See also Pamela Cooper-White, "The Pastor as Wounded Healer," chapter 8 in *The Cry of Tamar: Violence against Women and the Church's Response* (Minneapolis: Fortress, 2012). See especially her practical guidelines for clergy in "Staying Effective," 194-204.

Like many medical personnel of that time, her mother's doctor believed that withholding the terminal nature of the cancer was a benevolent choice. Feeling helpless and enraged by her father's insistence on this but bound by her loyalty to him, Weingarten was emotionally cut off from her mother for more than a year until an intern, not privy to the secret, conveyed the news to Weingarten's mother. During that year, Weingarten repeatedly argued with her father, urging him to let her speak about the cancer. Her father's response never varied. Each time she pleaded with him, he answered, "If she wants to know, she will ask." Weingarten eventually concluded that the real message the family sent to her mother during this time was that *they* could not tolerate her mother hearing the truth.[20] For years after her mother's death, Weingarten reflected on her family's dynamics, recognizing fully just how disempowered she had been, even while completely aware of the destructive power of secrets.[21] Weingarten came to see that she was in the *aware but disempowered* quadrant, the position that is most enervating to the witness. By identifying the forces in play — for example, her desire to spare her father pain while grieving the imminent loss of his wife; cultural attitudes that conferred expert status on the doctor, assuming that he knew best; her own desire to honor her mother's trust in her doctor — Weingarten was finally able to witness herself with compassion. All these things had silenced her during some of the most excruciating days of her life. Perhaps because of this experience and others like it, Weingarten created a conceptual framework to help others become conscious of their powerlessness so that they might find pathways toward both empowerment and awareness.

The pathos of this personal tragedy in Weingarten's life was preceded by an even more consequential vow of silence she had taken as a young child. The secret of her mother's cancer that tied her in knots as a young woman was subsequent to an earlier "secret" in which she was caught as a child in the 1950s. There Kaethe was a disempowered witness to her parents' ongoing political trauma. Her position as an (at least partially) aware but completely disempowered witness to her parents' fears affected her for decades. Having once overheard them speak of the man who had "stabbed them in the back" by reporting that they were Communists during the McCarthy era, Kaethe suffered nightmares in which a shadowy figure chased her, wielding a knife, ready to stab her in the back. Terrified, the child

---

20. Weingarten, *Common Shock*, 29. Page references to this work have been placed in the following text.

21. See page 57 in this book, note 30.

learned to fall asleep sitting with her back against the wall and spent her childhood years hypervigilant about every turn of political events. Though her mother had explained the outlines of the situation to Kaethe, she had asked her to promise never to mention it to her father, a request Kaethe honored for forty-six years (135). When Julius and Ethel Rosenberg were executed in 1953 "for conspiring to provide stolen atomic secrets to the Soviet Union" (136), Kaethe knew only that they, like her parents, were Communists. And they were killed. Having limited information, and determined never to break her promise, Kaethe lived in terror that the same fate would befall her parents. "Emotionally disconnected from my parents, relying on my own woefully inadequate resources, I collapsed. No one knew. I didn't tell. I kept silent. I was good" (138). Noting that the effects of this witnessing were both lifelong and life-shaping, she writes: "My parents' trauma was transferred to me through my witnessing it" (138).

These poignant stories anticipate still other personal narratives of common shock, especially those in which Weingarten or members of her immediate family suffered serious illness. She writes of the shock she experienced, for example, as a new mother when she was informed that her son had been born with a heart defect and might not live. (He did live.) A few years later, her daughter was born with a rare genetic abnormality that presaged a life of chronic disabilities. Weingarten herself has suffered breast cancer three times. In all these life circumstances, Weingarten grasps something of the interpersonal complexity of such witnessing when she writes: "I witnessed myself as a victim of breast cancer. Miranda [her daughter] witnessed me living with a life-threatening illness. Friends witnessed both of us. At each ring there is the potential for any of the four witness positions to be operative. One way of transforming the relational impasse of illness is to stay aware and active in relation to it, creating connections with others that everyone can bear" (79).

"Creating connections with others that everyone can bear." This is the thread that runs through all of Weingarten's essays, lectures, and articles. Again and again it is the community whose witness promises to uphold each individual in it. If a person has little or no community to call upon, the task at hand is to take action that will strengthen community ties. There is a great deal that human beings cannot bear alone, and Weingarten asserts that they do not have to bear it alone. She has spent her entire professional career helping others work through the very relational impasses that brought her such anguish as a child and young adult. The key to renewed life is to take trusted friends into one's confidence in times of crisis. The resilience and creativity of the community as a whole are what provide the wider and wider circles of support that are needed. In each situation, Weingarten threads her way forward, finding renewed determination to transform suffering into meaningful action. While acknowledging that illness and death can break one's heart, she attests that "it can be put back together" by breaking the silence and building sturdy connections with others (79).

Families that suffer ongoing health challenges need to add more and more witnesses in order to stay emotionally buoyed. Weingarten's daughter Miranda's rare genetic disorder and its unusual symptoms tended to isolate her from neighbors and peers. Together, mother and daughter found a way to educate their friends about the disorder and informed them of the specific kind of support they needed. Weingarten writes: "I proposed to Miranda that we design a ceremony and invite a group of friends and helpers whom she would trust to share the history of her living with her syndrome. . . . With [such an] audience, I hoped that she would also activate her own witness role in relation to this disorder . . . that she would no longer feel solely its victim" (83). Making her aim explicit, Miranda designed the invitation. She wrote: *"I am hoping that you will become members of an 'opposing despair/nourishing hope' team to help me deal with the ongoing trials of my life"* (83). Miranda also designed the ritual that followed. She gave each of the twelve people gathered a candle, and lit the one in front of her. "She began to tell her story. She asked people to light their candle from hers when they felt that they understood the magnitude of her experience. As people lit their candles one by one, at different intervals of time, she said she felt that 'each lit candle took some of the burden off me'" (83). This team provided the social support the family needed as they navigated one challenge after another related to Miranda's extraordinary needs. What began as a "team approach" to nourishing hope in the most intimate sphere of family life was reconceptualized for Weingarten's fellow family therapists.

In her article "Reasonable Hope: Construct, Clinical Applications, and Supports,"[22] Weingarten develops a conceptual framework for approaching devastating life circumstances. Desiring to make explicit what is often left implicit, she differentiates her definition of "reasonable" hope from other commonly accepted definitions of hope. Reasonable hope is not

---

22. Weingarten, "Reasonable Hope: Construct, Clinical Applications, and Supports," *Family Process* 49, no. 1 (2010). Page references to this work have been placed in the following text.

simply a *feeling* sustained by individuals, she insists, but rather is a *practice* sustained by an interdependent community. Reasonable hope doesn't exist as a "struggle against an uncertain, unknowable future" but instead perceives the future as "open, uncertain, and influenceable" (8). Persons with reasonable hope don't wait helplessly for a situation to change, but instead develop goals and seek specific strategies to meet them. And finally, reasonable hope is not a "black and white category" that admits no doubt or despair, but exists alongside contradictory feelings.

First, reasonable hope is relational. While recognizing that not all relationships are supportive of hope, Weingarten asserts that reasonable hope is best sustained by groups of people rather than by lone individuals. Drawing on Martin Buber's understanding of I-Thou relationships as well as Desmond Tutu's description of *ubuntu,* Weingarten maintains that conventional views of hope are too individualistic. Hope cannot be maintained apart from the willingness of others to care about one's suffering. Second, "reasonable hope is a practice; it is something we do with others . . . work[ing] together toward a preferred future." Weingarten says that this practice of "thinking of hope as a verb and not a noun" leads one toward communal action (8). Third, reasonable hope requires an attitude of expectancy toward a future that can be changed by actions undertaken in the present. Even when one cannot fully envision that future, hope is generated by concrete steps — especially those in the form of "creative communal synergies" undertaken now (9). Fourth, reasonable hope seeks to clarify realistic goals. It does not hope for the moon but for something that is concrete and doable. Hopelessness arises when one is overwhelmed and convinced that nothing that one does will help. As one scales back one's expectations and notices that even while one cannot do everything one can do something, goals and pathways into the future are formed. The process involves trial and error, perseverance, and an ability to notice when progress is being made, even very small steps toward one's goals. Finally, reasonable hope coexists with doubt and despair. If one assumes that despair cannot coexist alongside hope, one might ironically despair over one's very lack of hope, deeming it insufficient (10). With reasonable hope one learns to live in the midst of life's messiness and disappointments and to work with whatever is at hand.

Once these conceptual categories are in place, Weingarten illustrates them with clinical vignettes, demonstrating again the importance of learning to identify one's own witness position. Family therapists need to be both aware and empowered so they can cocreate conversations that allow

hope to arise, interview for resilience, and use questions that will activate reasonable hope. They need to identify barriers to reasonable hope
as well as possible sources of support, and to assess and remove possible
obstructions to love. Weingarten concludes the article by naming specific
practices that she believes would be supportive for anyone, but especially
for those colleagues who deal with seemingly intractable problems. She
writes: "Believe that the small is not trivial; accept proxy measures of success; register reasonable hope, welcome joy; enjoy vicarious hope; and
finally, embrace resistance" (19-22).

Weingarten personally embodies what she commends to others. She
has traveled to Croatia and South Africa, witnessing the suffering of communities devastated by war or AIDS, by racism or other forms of structural
violence. She writes about the intergenerational transmission of trauma,
as the impact of trauma in one generation is passed along to the next, especially among the poor and those most vulnerable in any society. Jewish
by heritage, she is particularly sensitive to the impact of the Holocaust
on subsequent generations. At times her exhortations toward her fellow
clinicians draw upon collective Jewish wisdom. She urges therapists to
welcome joy even in dire circumstances, to enjoy vicarious hope, and to
work for justice. "Resisting what is not just and pursuing what is just ac-
tivates and promotes reasonable hope" (22), she advises. Generations of
Jewish struggle for justice give historic weight to her witness.

To underscore the importance of human interdependence for healing
trauma, Weingarten draws on conceptions developed by Martin Buber
(I-Thou relationships), Desmond Tutu (an African understanding of
ubuntu), and Thich Nhat Hanh (a Buddhist concept of *interbeing*). While
there are nuances unique to each conception, all of them develop an understanding of human beings as being responsible, not only for themselves,
but also for others. They bring to mind, from a Christian perspective, the
paradox of the apostle Paul's injunction that we are each to bear the burdens of others while also bearing our own load. "Bear one another's burdens, and in this way you will fulfill the law of Christ," is followed three
verses later by "For all must carry their own loads" (Gal. 6:2, 5 NRSV).
The passage assumes that all persons are in danger of falling into temptation or despair. Thus, when we see another's need, we are to support him
in a spirit of gentleness, not deceiving ourselves that we are better than
others. While today a sister in Christ may be afflicted with fear and need
to be reminded to rest in God's love, tomorrow our own anxious rumina-
tions may need the compassionate presence of that very sister, in order to

restore our trust in the sufficiency of God's grace. Each person is to bear the burdens of others *and* is to carry one's own load. Bearing the burdens of others means reaching out to them with compassion. Carrying one's own load means taking responsibility for our own self-care, asking others for compassionate witnessing when we need it, and not setting ourselves up as somehow above needing the help of others. Being aware of our own needs for care, we are willing to turn to others, asking them to witness us while we give voice to our own sorrows and burdens. Mutual care is at the very heart of the church's life together in Christ.

When we consider Weingarten's concept of reasonable hope from a Christian standpoint, we first discover a surprising congruence between her concept of "reasonable hope" and a number of beliefs and practices in the church. First, as suggested above, Weingarten's understanding of human identity as corporate rather than individualistic is congruent with a New Testament depiction of the body of Christ as an interdependent community (as described by Paul in 1 Corinthians 12 and Romans 12 with the extended metaphor of our being members of a single body). Persons in community are members of one another who cannot pretend that they have no need of others. Just as each organ in the human body cannot function on its own, so each person in the community cannot function apart from every other person's contribution to the whole. Further, when one considers how members of the church are upheld by others in a time of crisis, one sees the kind of hope in action that Weingarten commends. Members of the church care for the afflicted by listening to their stories, praying for them, and offering them various kinds of practical help when needed. These small "but not trivial" actions inspire hope by offering support and care in a time of great vulnerability.

Based on an ethnographic study of what he describes as an "activist" congregation, Don Browning concludes that "the most meaningful part of care from the perspective of lay people is what they receive from one another in the informal and formal groups making up the ongoing life of the congregation," and not solely nor even primarily the pastoral care of the ordained clergy.[23] Just as Weingarten describes, persons are sustained in

23. Don Browning, "Pastoral Care and the Study of the Congregation," in *Beyond Clericalism: The Congregation as a Focus for Theological Education,* ed. Joseph C. Hough Jr. and Barbara G. Wheeler (Atlanta: Scholars Press, 1988), 117. The liturgical function and pastoral care of the clergy are crucial, however, in major life-cycle transitions, illness, and crisis. "The ministers don't have to be available all the time as long as they are available at the right time" (109).

hope even if in the present they have little access to feelings of hope. Hope functions more as a verb, a process or action, than as a feeling, a noun, or a personal attribute that one does or does not possess. In such circumstances it is common to hear members of the church attest that they are being upheld by the prayers of others. When they have no personal access to hope themselves, they rely on the hope of the community. Such a conviction resonates with Weingarten's notion of vicarious hope, in which the hope-filled actions of others buoy one up. Similarly, the ability to welcome joy even in painful situations echoes Paul's exhortation to "give thanks in all circumstances" (1 Thess. 5:18). Christian belief and practice are filled with instances of desolation and consolation existing side by side in the same life at the same time.

In practices of lament, despair and hope also exist side by side in the same breast. Indeed, it is one's faith in God that enables the believer to give voice to despair, which paradoxically claims hope at the same time.[24] Like Weingarten's depiction of reasonable hope, Christian hope is able to "accommodate doubt, contradictions and despair,"[25] not because it is reasonable but because it trusts in the power of a merciful God. Christian prayers of lament, so steeped in the psalms of the Hebrew Bible, not only provide a clear pathway to move through rage and shame into grief and mourning, they also help one discover courage and renewed trust even as one is filled with doubt and despair. In the prayer of lament, the psalmist cries out from a pit of shame, terror, and despair to a God as close as his own breath. Time after time, he is delivered against all odds and lives to praise God with heart and voice.

Unlike Weingarten's conception of "reasonable hope," however, the church is anchored in a transcendent hope, one that might be deemed *un*reasonable by the world. God's miraculous grace and steadfast love is preached every Sunday of the year. While those in personal crisis may not themselves fully trust it for a long, dark season of their lives, they are nevertheless reminded of it in story, creed, ritual, sermon, image, and song week after week. The biblical narrative of divine intervention — of manna in the wilderness, of angels descending with glad tidings, of prophets taken up into heaven in chariots of fire — feeds the church's imagination for all that is impossible, unreasonable, and hope beyond hope, and anchors it in a ground utterly beyond its own making. Each person is given opportu-

24. See also chapter 5 of this volume.
25. Weingarten, "Reasonable Hope," 10.

nities to find her unique life story in a larger story that began long before she was born and that will continue long after she has departed this world because it is a divine story. It is the story of God with us. Each person's own life's saga, when set narratively within that divine saga, gives rise to the community's hope.

Like those who live without faith, those in the church know that their lives are precarious and that the future is unknowable. Weingarten states that "the future is not determined but is influenceable . . . that we can join with others, that creative communal synergies can happen . . . that spontaneous actions . . . arise from collective commitments."[26] To one rooted and grounded in biblical hope, these words sound remarkably similar to a description of God's gracious providence. Yet, for persons of faith, the future is influenceable because *God* is influenceable. We may indeed hope for creative communal synergies to arise, but any trust we put in human action is bracketed by a larger trust in God. That is why the church is constant in prayer. Don Saliers writes:

> Suppose we regard the sustained practice of the Christian life as a continual intercessory prayer, and a willingness not to claim too much for God on our own terms. Life as intercession — in word and action — is a constant holding of the world in all its suffering and tragedy before God. Such intercession requires both lament and doxology. . . . The difference between drowning in the tragedy of the world and turning toward the slow work of God is discerned in the witness of those whose lives embody lament, intercession and praise. . . . Taking the passion of Christ and the continuing suffering of the world as the matrix of authentic spirituality implies that the suffering life of Christ is encountered ever anew in history.[27]

As in Weingarten's picture of reasonable hope, those who hope in God seek goals and give thanks for pathways that open before them. But unlike Weingarten, the church relies not solely on a community of caring individuals, but more fundamentally on a belief in the Compassionate One, the source of all human compassion.

---

26. Weingarten, "Reasonable Hope," 5.

27. Don Saliers, "The Bitter Christ: Suffering and Spirituality in Denial," *Spiritus: A Journal of Christian Spirituality* 10, no. 2 (Fall 2010): 294-303. *Spiritus* is published by the Johns Hopkins University Press.

Weingarten encourages her fellow family therapists to engage in "a daily practice of awe" in order to find ongoing inspiration for the task of helping others rebuild their lives in the wake of trauma or tragedy. Such a practice also finds parallels in the Christian life. For example, members of the church are encouraged to read Scripture regularly, to praise God for the good gifts of creation and redemption, and to ponder "any excellence [and] anything worthy of praise" (Phil. 4:8). Indeed, at several points Weingarten's exhortations seem to echo the very things that Scripture attests will enable a community not to be "overcome by evil, but [to] overcome evil with good" (Rom. 12:21), or to "do justice, and to love kindness, and to walk humbly with [its] God" (Mic. 6:8). From a standpoint in Christian belief, such practices cannot be understood apart from their transcendent grounding in the compassion of a God who actively sustains the community by the grace that continually pours out upon it.

In preparing students for ministry, Andrew Purves reminds them that "to suffer with another is still to suffer . . . [and that] compassion will increase our experience of suffering. We can buckle under the weight of accumulated pain."[28] Noting that suffering has the capacity to "cut the ground out from under our feet,"[29] Purves, like Weingarten, does not romanticize suffering nor commend it for its possible spiritual benefits.[30] He knows that one can become overwhelmed and can shut down one's openness toward others in order to reduce the impact of the pain. Instead, he asks what makes it possible to continue to be willing to respond to others with care and compassion. "Compassion," Purves writes, "is deeply rooted in the life of God as revealed to us in Jesus Christ."[31] We cannot engage in such a ministry if it is grounded in the shallow soil of our own spiritual strength. "A compassionate ministry must be grounded in God and God's own compassion for the world."[32] Such an axiomatic standpoint reframes

28. Andrew Purves, *The Search for Compassion: Spirituality and Ministry* (Louisville: Westminster John Knox, 1989), 83.

29. Purves, *The Search for Compassion,* 83.

30. Weingarten writes: "I do not subscribe to the idea that suffering can be redeemed. Rather, I believe suffering is always terrible, often tragic. I do not believe that suffering serves a purpose, although many people, and I am one, have used suffering to serve a purpose. . . . Cancer brought me nothing but *tsuris,* the Yiddish for trouble. I, on the other hand, worked mightily hard to make some good come of it, for myself and others." *Common Shock,* 231.

31. Purves, *The Search for Compassion,* 12.

32. Purves, *The Search for Compassion,* 28.

and reconfigures Weingarten's model of compassionate witnessing, placing it into an explicitly Christian context.

God alone can bear the sins of the world and not be destroyed by them. God alone can fully witness the horror and the terror of what human beings are capable of inflicting on one another. In Jesus Christ, God takes the suffering of the world into his own capacious heart and ministers, openly or secretly, through the Holy Spirit to every creature in distress. While God calls human witnesses to partake in this ministry, it is first and foremost God's ministry into which human beings are called to participate. It is God's Spirit who opens human hearts to hear and to respond to the suffering of others. It is not something that human beings are capable of by their own power. Purves's definition of pastoral theology is pertinent here. He writes: "Pastoral theology is understood properly first of all as a theology of the care of God for us in, through, and as Jesus Christ. . . . Only secondarily, derivatively, and above all, participatively, . . . is pastoral theology an account of the pastoral work of the church."[33] The church's capacity for staying open to others depends fundamentally on its faithfulness in listening to God and on its turning to God for daily sustenance, guidance, inspiration, and nurture. If the church is not to be grounded in the shallow soil of its own spiritual strength, it needs constantly to hear God's Word of hope. Purves comments: "We have to live the theological reality of new life in Christ in such a way that we are always being healed. Either we are being healed of our own suffering or compassion will become increasingly impossible for us."[34] As those in the church are healed of their own suffering, they may grow in creativity, resilience, and personal strength even in the midst of trial and affliction, what has been called "post-traumatic growth" in the psychological literature.[35] Post-traumatic growth is not a return to a pretrauma existence, but it gives evidence of a new identity and a new narrative. Strength and resilience replace powerlessness and being overwhelmed. Even so, Christian hope cannot simply be equated with posttraumatic hope. It functions within a different conceptual matrix than any psychological concept. By definition, it entails claims to truth that do not function at an empirical level. While Weingarten's "reasonable hope" can

---

33. Andrew Purves, *Reconstructing Pastoral Theology: A Christological Foundation* (Louisville: Westminster John Knox, 2004), xviii.

34. Purves, *The Search for Compassion*, 84.

35. See, for example, R. G. Tedeshi and L. G. Calhoun, *Posttraumatic Growth: Conceptual Foundation and Empirical Evidence* (Philadelphia: Lawrence Erlbaum Associates, 2004).

be embraced by the church in a penultimate sense, it needs to be lodged within an ultimate framework of faith in God's action on our behalf and for our sake. In this context, Weingarten's concept of witnessing reclaims the ancient meaning of religious testimony. Examples of such testimony pervade Nicholas Wolterstorff's reflections in his book *Lament for a Son*.

> Suffering may do us good — may be a blessing, something to be thankful for. This I have learned. . . . Suffering is the shout of "No" by one's whole existence to that over which one suffers — the shout of "No" by nerves and gut and gland and heart to pain, to death, to injustice, to depression, to hunger, to humiliation, to bondage, to abandonment. And sometimes, when the cry is intense, there emerges a radiance which elsewhere seldom appears: a glow of courage, of love, of insight, of self-lessness, of faith. In that radiance we see best what humanity was meant to be. . . . In the valley of suffering, despair and bitterness are brewed. But there also character is made. The valley of suffering is the vale of soul-making.[36]

Those whose souls have been made in such a deep vale are called by God to minister to others with the compassion they have come to know and trust (2 Cor. 1:3-5).[37]

---

36. Nicholas Wolterstorff, *Lament for a Son* (Grand Rapids: Eerdmans, 1987), 96-97.

37. In *Spirit and Trauma* Shelly Rambo seems to deny anything that might be characterized as "post-traumatic growth," instead suggesting that the best one can do is "remain" in the wake of trauma. Divine love does not triumph over death. "Instead, divine love survives" (170). Maybe the most one can claim is that the Christian story tells of a "divine remaining, the story of love that survives . . . a cry arising from the abyss." She ends her book by asking, "The question is: can we witness it?"

CHAPTER 3

Christian Forgiveness

....

Healing the Emotional Wounds of Childhood

Are adults who were abused by their parents when they were children obligated to forgive them? When an adult Christian undergoes therapy and begins to recover memories of painful abuse that are at the very heart of her suffering, and when she realizes that those who abused her were none other than her own parents, is she still obliged to "honor them in the Lord"? If she actually confronts her parents and they minimize or deny their culpability, is she justified in cutting them off, in turning away from them and having nothing further to do with them? Or must she forgive their trespasses against her, knowing as she does the unfathomable depth of the mercy and forgiveness of God toward her own sins? If she attempts to forgive them, what is she to do with her rage and outrage, with the feelings of hurt and betrayal that keep emerging? Questions like these burden those who seek to heal from the emotional wounds of childhood and to live faithful lives of Christian discipleship. For innumerable Christians, these questions are not merely theoretical, but have tremendous practical implications for their most intimate relationships and for the living out of their faith. In this chapter I want to examine a nexus of questions about the nature of forgiveness with this particular situation in mind: the adult who is seeking to heal from genuine harm committed by his parents when he was a child. What is the relationship between the healing he seeks and a Christian understanding of forgiveness? I ask this question as a Reformed pastoral theologian who, as a practicing pastoral counselor, has faced the question of human forgiveness in many guises.

I begin with a description of what I mean by parental abuse, particularly because, as Marie Fortune has observed, the word "abuse" is sometimes used so loosely that anything that is considered harmful or that lowers a person's self-esteem is labeled abusive, making the term too broad to be helpful.[1] First, situations of abuse are those "which are dominated by fear"[2] where, in the case of physical abuse, parents subject their children to physical violence and use force, threats, and intimidation to make their children obey them. Second, children who grow up in homes where they are sexually violated are victims of incestuous abuse. Sexual abuse would include not only sexual touching of the child, but also having the child touch the parent sexually. It would also include sexualized talk, showing a child pornographic materials, or some kind of intentional parental exhibitionism in front of the child.[3] Third, the phenomenon of psychological abuse is "a pattern which occurs over time and which instills in that person a sense of their worthlessness and their inability to take care of themselves."[4] Repeated shaming and humiliating comments, efforts at keeping the child totally in control (basically not seeing the child as a separate person with a will of her own), while attempting to isolate the child from outside sources of help, all contribute to this kind of abuse. Such patterns of psychological abuse are familiar to us from literature on cults (which we think of as "brainwashing"), as members are systematically taught not to trust their own perceptions and thus lose their capacity for independent judgment and initiative and become dominated by fear and dependency.[5] The suffering of persons subjected to extensive psychological abuse has also been compared to the anguish of hostages and prisoners of war.[6]

Perhaps it goes without saying that all such abuse, whether physical, sexual, or psychological, is sinful. It is impossible to overestimate the damage done to children; such wounding leaves lasting scars, sometimes completely debilitating them. Children are to be cherished as gifts from God,

---

1. Marie Fortune, "The Nature of Abuse," *Pastoral Psychology* 41 (1993): 275-88.

2. Fortune, "The Nature of Abuse," 276.

3. Mic Hunter, *Abused Boys: The Neglected Victims of Sexual Abuse* (New York: Fawcett Columbine, 1990), 8-9.

4. Fortune, "The Nature of Abuse," 277.

5. Cf. Steven Hassan, *Combatting Cult Mind Control* (Rochester, Vt.: Park Street Press, 1988), 55-56. Hassan makes a distinction between "brainwashing," which is a coercive process undertaken by an enemy, and "mind control," which is a more subtle process involving hypnotic techniques undertaken by one perceived to be a friend or peer. In the latter case, the victim participates in his own victimization as information that he voluntarily gives is used to manipulate or deceive him.

6. Fortune, "The Nature of Abuse," 277. See also Margaret Z. Kornfeld, *Cultivating Wholeness: A Guide to Care and Counseling in Faith Communities* (New York: Continuum, 1999), 262.

not abused, hurt, or in any way wounded by those whose God-given calling is to raise, guide, nurture, and protect them. To inflict any kind of abuse upon a small child, whose very life depends upon its parents, quite rightly evokes strong feelings of moral outrage. Such abusive behavior not only clearly betrays a gross failure to love one's nearest neighbor, but more fundamentally indicates a gaping abyss between the person engaging in such abuse and God. The distortion and rupture in the abuser's primary relationship with God have disastrous effects on his interpersonal relationships with those in his family. Such sin is particularly disconcerting in the context of the parent/child relationship because that relationship is meant to shower God's own blessing on children. Recall that through their relationship with their parents, children are given God's express promise of blessing. The fifth commandment reads, "Honor your father and your mother, as the LORD your God commanded you; that your days may be prolonged, and that it may go well with you, in the land which the LORD your God gives you" (Deut. 5:16). In explicating the obedience, honor, and gratitude that children owe their parents, Calvin emphasizes that since God himself places parents in authority over them, "it makes no difference whether they [the parents] are worthy or unworthy of this honor."[7] But he goes on to say that

> we ought in passing to note that we are bidden to obey our parents only in the Lord (Eph. 6:1). This is apparent from the principle already laid down. For they sit in that place to which they have been advanced by the Lord, who shares with them a part of his honor. Therefore, the submission paid to them ought to be a step toward honoring that highest Father. Hence, if they spur us to transgress the law we have a perfect right to regard them not as parents, but as strangers who are trying to lead us away from obedience to our true Father.[8]

"We have a perfect right to regard them not as parents, but as strangers." Parents who dishonor God by abusing their children are putting their children in terrible jeopardy, the worst of which may be in undermining their trust in God. In today's world, we have plenty of evidence showing how abusive fathers can lead their children into questioning the very goodness of God. Certain contemporary feminist readings of the gospel,

---

7. John Calvin, *Institutes of the Christian Religion* 2.8.36, ed. John T. McNeill, vol. 1 (Philadelphia: Westminster, 1960), 402.

8. Calvin, *Institutes* 2.8.38, pp. 403-4.

for instance, call the loving Fatherhood of God into question because of the abusive practices of human fathers.[9] But Calvin's argument is based on diametrically opposite presuppositions. He assumes that since God is the true Father, all human fathers (and mothers) are but pale and distant reflections of that Fatherhood. Human parents who reflect the light and goodness of God's Fatherhood (that is, the watchful providential care of his children) are worthy of their children's honor precisely because they point beyond themselves to God, the One parents and their children are both called to honor. It is not that an abusive father is capable of calling into question the goodness of God as Father, but rather that God calls into question the fatherhood of that parent who abuses his children. Karl Barth takes a line of thought similar to Calvin's:

> No human father, but God alone, is properly, truly and primarily Father. No human father is the creator of his child, the controller of its destiny, or its savior from sin, guilt and death. No human father is by his word the source of its temporal and eternal life. In this proper, true and primary sense, God — and He alone — is Father. He is so as the Father of mercy, as the Father of His Son, of the Lord Jesus Christ. But it is of this Father's grace that, in correspondence to His own, there should exist a human fatherhood also. And the fact that the latter may symbolize the fatherhood of God in a human and creaturely form is what lends it its meaning and value and entitles it to respect.[10]

Though children seeking to honor God might justly regard their parents as strangers, doing so entails serious problems. First, because of the way we grow psychologically and develop as human beings, it is literally impossible to sever this primary relationship. Second, when we view the parent/child relationship in the context of the intergenerational family system, any attempt at cutting off a member only exacerbates the problem, not only for the victim, but also for the entire extended family. And third, cutting another off in this way actually reinforces a pattern of mutual alienation, hostility, and lack of trust. Nevertheless, it seems humanly impossible that anyone could forgive this kind of violence.

9. See, for example, Joanne Carlson Brown and Rebecca Parker, "For God So Loved the World?" in *Christianity, Patriarchy, and Abuse: A Feminist Critique*, ed. Carole R. Bohn and Joanne C. Brown (Cleveland: Pilgrim Press, 1989), 1-30.

10. Karl Barth, *Church Dogmatics* III/4 (Edinburgh: T. & T. Clark, 1961), 245.

Those little acquainted with the effects of childhood abuse sometimes have difficulty imagining the extent of the suffering caused by it and may consequently minimize its impact. A great deal of additional harm is done, however, if such persons recommend that the sufferer "forgive and forget," or suggest that she should not spend so many useless hours solipsistically focusing on past events that she can't change anyway. Such comments have the effect of shaming the person for doing the one thing that might actually bring some healing, namely, paying attention to the effects of the trauma in her life and allowing herself to feel the profound grief related to it. Minimizing the extent of another's suffering seems to be a perennial temptation on the part of helpers, simply because being willing to acknowledge the magnitude of the harm is so painful. Some have aptly called it "soul murder."[11]

To provide a particular focus to our discussion, let me describe the situation of a woman who sought psychotherapy in adulthood in order to heal from having been raped by her father when she was three. Like most persons healing from sexual abuse, it took her many years even to learn the nature of her most intimate suffering, for she had repressed all memory of the traumatic event as a way to survive. I will not quote her description of the rape (once she recovered her memory of it), but rather of its protracted effects as she was growing up. While each person's experience is unique, the kinds of symptoms and experiences Gizelle (a pseudonym) describes are characteristic for persons who have undergone traumatic sexual abuse.

> The effects of the abuse manifested through my body. I sleepwalked. I had high fevers that were life threatening. And they could never find a cause. I had nightmares. I had severe asthma. I would just stop breathing. I was at the doctor's all the time. I was in the bed, always sick. My legs were turned out so badly that I could not walk without tripping over my own feet. I had to wear corrective shoes. It all fits now.
>
> I split my father into two different people, because there was no other way to sit across the breakfast table from him. The man who came down and sat at the kitchen table was my father. The man who came in the middle of the night and molested me was a shadow. I made him into someone else.
>
> And as I split him into two, I split myself into two. There was the little

---

11. Leonard Shengold, *Soul Murder: The Effects of Childhood Abuse and Deprivation* (New York: Ballantine Books, 1991).

girl whose father taught her to ride a bike, who got A's and became a perfectionist. And then there was the little girl who played in the attic, felt that she was dying, wanted to commit suicide, had nightmares. But I never could speak of her. Her voice had been taken away.

I felt caught, trapped in my body. That's continued into adulthood. I never heard any messages from my body. I would be really sick and I'd stagger around and go to work. I made a lifetime dedication of not listening to my body, because if I had, I would have had to hear that I was raped, and I couldn't do that and survive.

I developed an eating disorder when I was eighteen, which they now call anorexia nervosa. I was at college. I felt obese if I weighed over ninety-five pounds.[12]

Gizelle's travail continued as an adult.

I remember very distinctly that when my daughter was the age I had been when I was raped, I began to distance myself from her. She came to me in tears and said, "Mommy, you don't like me anymore." I didn't remember the rape at all. When Adrienne was five, I developed chronic hip and back problems. I became crippled by the pain. I had anxiety attacks so bad I couldn't move. I was in severe depression. One morning when I was thirty-eight and my daughter was almost twelve, I took a lot of pills. I never said anything to anybody. I just knew I couldn't go on in the kind of pain I was in, that I had tried everything I could think of. As I said, it was not just the physical pain, but the terror that hooked into the physical pain. The two completely overwhelmed me.[13]

Gizelle tried to commit suicide on four different occasions. Her last attempt very nearly succeeded. After recovering from the fourth attempt, she sought therapy. After a long and arduous process, she was eventually able to remember what had happened to her nearly forty years earlier. She experienced immense relief once she was able to bring it to conscious awareness.

Since it's come out, it's been the difference of night and day, of living in hell and living on the earth. For so much of my life, I have fought death

12. Ellen Bass and Laura Davis, *The Courage to Heal: A Guide for Women Survivors of Child Sexual Abuse* (New York: Harper and Row, 1988), 448-49.

13. Bass and Davis, *The Courage to Heal,* 449-50.

wishes. Now I feel grounded, very connected to the earth, very deter-mined to stay. My strength and energy to deal with my life is returning. My neck has begun to unlock. I've begun to feel a looseness in my hips that I never felt before. I really can't tell you how far my body can heal. But I do know that I will heal physically enough to be able to lead a productive, full, and happy life, even if I have residual pain.[14]

While symptoms of physical and psychological abuse may differ from those specific to sexual abuse, all three types of abuse can be severe enough to lead to suicide.

How might someone like Gizelle heal from trauma of such immensity? What steps would she need to take to find any kind of peace or wholeness or restoration? Would forgiving her father be a necessary step for her to become fully healed? Would it somehow help promote her healing pro-cess? Or is it rather the converse, that emotional healing would somehow facilitate her ability to forgive? Or are healing and forgiveness not related to each other in either of these ways? If not, how then are they related?

Two contemporary schools of psychological thought may help us think about the issues of healing, forgiveness, and reconciliation. One school is more oriented toward the internal dynamics of the self while the other is more oriented toward the outer relationship with the parents. Both perspectives provide insight into the question of forgiveness insofar as it is a matter of human growth and maturity. That is to say, being able truly to forgive a person is, among other things, a matter of a certain measure of psychological maturity. The first approach, known generally as "family systems," focuses on the wider implications of abuse, both its origins and its consequences, for the extended family. Any "symptom," such as abuse, comes into being over a period of generations, so that an adequate theory must take into account more than one generation. Family systems theory may be especially pertinent to the church, not only because the church itself is obviously a system that can be analyzed, but even more because the theory can facilitate a glimpse into the communal nature of sin, into the ways that sin arises in specific relational contexts and involves a vast hidden web of complex circumstances and relationships. Just as grace is passed from one generation to another, as God blesses persons through families rich in love, so also is sin mysteriously visited on children and children's children unto the third and fourth generation. Family systems

14. Bass and Davis, *The Courage to Heal*, 456.

theory, when placed into a Christian theological context, enables a glimpse into the hidden truth of our human solidarity in both sin and grace.

The second approach, known generally as "object relations" theory, has to do with the developmental process each of us undergoes as infants, as we learn in our earliest years about love and hate, guilt and reparation, and as we respond to both the gratifications and the frustrations of being completely dependent upon another human being to meet all our needs. This theory is pertinent to our subject, not only because it shows the psychological capacities needed for forgiveness to take place, but also because of its specific focus on the relationship between children and parents.

Learning to forgive our parents has enormous implications for our emotional and spiritual growth, perhaps more than any other relationship we have, for the simple reason that our parents are internalized parts of our own personality in a unique sense. Achieving a more harmonious relationship with our parents in the outer world simultaneously affects our inner world as well, that is, our relationship to ourselves. If we experience forgiving our actual mother and father for the hurt they caused us, the internalized representations of our parents would also change, allowing for less need to split off or repress painful aspects of the self. Our "inner" parents would become far less persecuting and more supportive as a consequence. While such psychological concepts, though very important, are not sufficient for understanding the complexity of what is involved in the event of forgiveness, at least not from a Christian perspective, they can nevertheless help illuminate certain crucial features. I will first look at a family systems approach by drawing on the work of Murray Bowen, and then turn to an object relations perspective, drawing on the work of Melanie Klein, before putting both into a theological framework.[15]

The first step many survivors of abuse take is a literal one away from the abuser; that is to say, they put as much distance between themselves and their parents as is physically possible. Angry, hurt, betrayed, and at last free of the household where the abuse took place, they are eager to begin a life of their own as far away from that home as possible. Particularly in a mobile society like the United States, a decision to distance themselves from their family of origin and simply cut off contact has not only been possible but, by the advice given by much popular therapeutic

---

15. I am greatly indebted to a book by David W. Augsburger, *Helping People Forgive* (Louisville: Westminster John Knox, 1996), in which Augsburger features each of these psychological theories in relation to its implications for the process of forgiveness.

"self-help," has also been widespread. Thus bonds of kinship already frayed by economic considerations that take grown children to faraway locations are further strained as children intentionally distance themselves, both physically and emotionally, from their parents and siblings. In the cultural ethos of the United States since the late 1960s, there have been advocates for this kind of radical dismembering of the family. Cutting off their parents, seeking to dissociate themselves from a "dysfunctional" family, and avoiding the "toxic" relationships of their family of origin have all been recommended to survivors of abuse as ways of coping with its ongoing painful effects. Underlying such recommendations is an implicit portrait of emotional maturity as a matter of separateness and autonomy. "Maturity is ending dysfunctional relationships, writing off controlling persons, distancing from dominating people, getting out of trapped or manipulative relationships, becoming an autonomous self-reliant individual with freedom from co-dependence."[16]

Murray Bowen and other family systems therapists, however, would strongly contest such an understanding of emotional maturity. Human maturity for Bowen is not a matter of becoming more and more "independent" or autonomous, but rather a matter of growing from the infant's original emotional fusion with his mother toward becoming a fully differentiated self in relation to those in his family. A mature, differentiated adult would be capable of taking a clear "I" stand while remaining emotionally linked to significant others; that is to say, he would be able to stand alone and claim who he is while also remaining closely connected to those he loves. He is differentiated from others without being separated, cut off, or isolated from them. This is more difficult to do than it might at first seem. It is difficult to state with conviction what one believes, thinks, feels, and values in a clearly differentiated way to those with whom one is emotionally close, particularly when one's feelings, ideas, and values are unlike those of others in the family. The "togetherness forces" in a family exert strong pressure either to "fuse" with others, blending one's own values and identity in with theirs, or are so strong that one feels compelled to distance oneself by reactively taking an opposite position. Staying connected to one's family is a matter of knowing how to stay centered and nonanxious, how to interact nonreactively with family members, especially when "taboo" topics are raised, those issues that arouse shame, guilt, anxiety, or grief. Those in

---

16. Augsburger, *Helping People Forgive*, 47. This sentence does not represent Augsburger's own view of maturity, but rather is his depiction of how some people conceive of it.

the family who are anxious about human separateness would tend to gloss over differences. In situations of conflict or anxiety, they would seek to reestablish some kind of emotional fusion.[17] Those anxious about human closeness would seek to distance themselves from others or to cut them off as a way of dealing with the anxiety involved in being in a conflictual or painful relationship with them. The goal of human maturity would be a position midway between these two poles of moving compulsively either toward or away from intimate others. Those who are emotionally mature would be able to tolerate the anxiety of being close to others without losing their identity, on the one hand, and the anxiety of being separate from others without feeling isolated or abandoned, on the other.

When confronted with another's hurt or anger, those who normally distance themselves under stress would tend to give an account or offer an explanation, in an effort to excuse any wrongdoing, rather than facing it frankly and acknowledging it openly. By contrast, those whose anxiety is activated by separateness would tend to appease or placate the other, negate any rightful claims they may have, and generally give up their own point of view as a way of seeking reconciliation at any cost. Fully mature adults, in contrast to both of these positions, would be able to take responsibility for their own point of view, values, and actions, and could stand up for them vigorously, but could also openly admit it when they have acted contrary to their values and apologize to whomever they have hurt. When entering into a process of reconciliation with one they have harmed, they would attempt neither to appease the other nor to exonerate themselves, but would be capable of offering a true apology. A true apology "offers no defense or excuse, gives true sorrow or regret for the injury, pledges full change in a clear appeal to the whole person [and involves] a painful embracing of [their] deeds and their consequences."[18]

By definition, families in which abuse has occurred do not have clear boundaries safeguarding each member's physical and emotional space. Human closeness is experienced as being extremely dangerous because to be close *means* to be violated. Therefore, in such families the temptation to move compulsively away from the other is very great indeed. Unfortunately, cutting off from the family of origin not only fails to resolve the problem of how to cope with intimacy but also transfers it

---

17. Augsburger, *Helping People Forgive,* 42.

18. Augsburger, *Helping People Forgive,* 42. The chart on this page vividly differentiates these three options sought by those attempting to reconcile with one another.

to the next generation. When such compulsive distance is maintained between an adult and her extended family, "the cutoff tends to make emotional forces in the nuclear family system implosive, with the result that the reactivity of its members becomes more automatic."[19] Cutoffs in one generation have the effect of increasing overall family anxiety and intensifying emotional fusion in the following generation. When abused children become adults and cut off relationships with their families of origin, the unresolved emotional issues that belong with their parents unwittingly get transferred in some form to their children. This transfer process usually happens outside of their awareness. If they are distant or detached from their family of origin, for example, they would likely become overly invested in and emotionally enmeshed with their own children, making it difficult for the children to grow normally. They would likely feel engulfed by the overcloseness of their parent, and would typically react by disconnecting and pulling away, thus perpetuating the cycle for yet another generation. Cutting off parents apparently does not resolve the relational impasse; it merely displaces it. Augsburger asks several questions that go right to the heart of the matter: "If the frozen grief is denied and mourning is displaced onto subsequent generations, what will be the new shape of this system? How will the pain trickle down? With what long-range increase in enmeshment? What payments will be charged to the children, what emotional story of repetition without reparation, recapitulation without reconciliation [will] be turned in a new direction?"[20] It is an observable psychological phenomenon that whatever is not emotionally confronted and worked through in one generation will be passed on to the next. "Repetition compulsion," or being compelled to repeat unconsciously what cannot be faced consciously, does not happen simply in the lives of isolated individuals. It is rather an intergenerational, complex social reality.

> If parents fail to do this [embrace their own unconscious wounds], they unwittingly pass on the weight of unhealed suffering to their children. It is not the psychic wounds of the parents which are, themselves, toxic to the children, but the lack of conscious encounter with those wounds that pervades the family unconscious and gets transferred to the next

19. Edwin H. Friedman, *Generation to Generation: Family Process in Church and Synagogue* (New York: Guilford Press, 1985), 26.
20. Augsburger, *Helping People Forgive*, 30-31.

generation. If the previous generation hasn't consciously suffered, the pain will be handed on, often unconsciously, to the next generation.[21]

Lasting resolution, it would seem, happens only when adult children decide to confront the impasse with their parents, only when they stop running away and face the depths of their own pain. And because the pain from the abuse is both an interpersonal and an intrapersonal phenomenon, it can be approached either externally or internally.

Let us turn, then, to an intrapsychic perspective on the same set of issues. From an object relations point of view, "reconciliation . . . comes about as a result of peacemaking *within* — resolving intrapersonal relationships — leading to peacemaking *between* in personal harmony."[22] Intrapsychically, reconciliation with our parents is an event that is unique in kind because the very building blocks of our psychic makeup are the primary internalized objects of our mother and father. Given the way we develop as human beings, the internalization of our parents inevitably forms an integral part of our identity. Our peculiar psychology is substantively shaped by what we have introjected of our parents (assuming that they were our primary caregivers), by what we have taken of them into ourselves, into our own sense of self. We piece together an identity by internalizing them, their way of speaking, their way of holding and feeding us, and our feelings about how they move and smell and taste. We drink in their eyes and the way they look at us. We become finely attuned to their emotional state of being. We absorb everything about them and weave fantasies about everything they do (or fail to do) from the earliest beginnings of our lives. If we later turn away from them and reject them because they have hurt us, we are also thereby rejecting and "cutting off" an essential part of ourselves. The distinctively Christian perception that we "are members one of another" is applicable not to our ecclesiology alone. In an analogous way, it is also a profound psychological truth pertaining to what it means to live in a family, to have a mother and a father whom we have internalized even before we consciously knew who they were. Melanie Klein describes this process of internalization as follows:

> The baby, having incorporated the parents, feels them to be live people inside its body in the concrete way in which deep unconscious phanta-

---

21. Phillip Bennett, "Family Complexes and Individuation," *Round Table Review* 1, no. 5 (May-June 1994): 9.

22. Augsburger, *Helping People Forgive*, 53.

sies are experienced — they are, in its mind, "internal" or "inner" objects, as I have termed them. Thus an inner world is being built up in the child's unconscious mind, corresponding to actual experiences and impressions gained from people and the external world, and yet altered by its own phantasies and impulses. If it is a world of people predominantly at peace with each other and with the ego, inner harmony, security and integration ensue.[23]

The reverse of Klein's statement is unfortunately also true. If the world we internalize is one where the people are predominantly at war with each other and with us, then inner disharmony, insecurity, and disintegration or splitting occur. Because the normal process of human bonding and attachment entails the psychic introjection of our parents, our relationship with them occupies a unique place in our psychology. They become the prototype or template, so to speak, of all subsequent relationships. Working things through with our parents therefore has the potential to affect all our relationships profoundly, even our relationship with ourselves. Because the internalized image of our parents is so formative of our own sense of self, we are mistaken if we think we can rid ourselves of our parents simply by putting the distance of time or space between them and us. Decades, indeed a whole lifetime, can go by without seeing them, but our relationship with them will not cease to live on inside our own minds. Even if we have consciously "forgotten" them, they are nevertheless operative and present to us unconsciously, that is, outside of our awareness. Insofar as we successfully dissociate ourselves from them inwardly, all that we actually accomplish is to split them off from our ego awareness; unfortunately, in doing so we also cut off any possibility for growth, change, or healing to take place in relation to them.

From an intrapsychic perspective, a person needs to reach a certain minimal level of emotional maturity to have the psychological capacity to forgive. In Klein's understanding of normal development, every infant goes through stages from a phase of primary attachment where the mother and infant are one and the mother is internalized as all good (ages one to three months, the so-called schizoid position), to a second phase where the mother and infant begin to separate and the mother begins to be split into good and bad (four to six months, the so-called paranoid position). In this

23. Melanie Klein, *Love, Guilt, and Reparation, and Other Works, 1921-1945* (New York: Free Press, 1975), 312-13, cited by Augsburger, *Helping People Forgive*, 54.

second phase of development, the baby experiences intense love toward the gratifying object and intense hate toward the frustrating object, not yet realizing that they are one and the same person. Just as the emotions split, so also does the mother; she is perceived by the infant as the idealized "good" mother, who satisfies her every need, on the one hand, and the persecuting "bad" mother, who frustrates the infant in her wishes and desires, on the other. Finally, if all goes well, the infant is able to achieve the so-called depressive position (at about age six months to three years) when she can perceive the mother as a unified whole, at once the persecuting "bad" mother and the gratifying "good" one. And just as the mother is eventually perceived as a whole person, so the child also begins to experience herself as a separate whole person with contradictory feelings toward one and the same mother. "When love and hate are experienced together, a new set of feelings emerges for the first time: guilt, sadness, depression, and grief: guilt that one's hostile feelings have hurt the other, sadness at the loss, grief and depression in consequence. This emotional position — the depressive position — makes possible feelings of concern."[24]

The transition to the depressive position is what enables the child to make reparations to the parent. The infant becomes anxious that her hate may be too powerful for the parent, that her bad feelings will outweigh the good ones and she may even have the power to annihilate her mother's goodness. If the mother survives the infant's destructive impulses and fantasies and does not retaliate, but continues to love and nurture the child, then feelings of gratitude and love will well up in the child. The child would then wish to repair any damage she has done in her imagination and would desire to reconcile her mother to herself, safeguarding "the good object" outside her and restoring the good object representation within. As the infant's earliest experience of the mother's forgiveness, this primitive psychological process forms the rudimentary underpinnings of the adult capacity to forgive. The child who has this kind of experience with a mother in the earliest months of life will have the psychological capacity for building relationships where forgiveness is emotionally possible.

> True reparation, rising out of psychic realities between infant and mother, allows the experiencing of real pain and grief and a genuine desire to reshape the inner world of love, hate, and guilt into a new unity and to respond to the external reality in bonding ways. . . . Authentic for-

24. Augsburger, *Helping People Forgive,* 57; see also figure 3.2, p. 58.

giveness . . . is marked by a reconciliation in which there is movement by both parties toward each other, cessation of continuing animosity over the injury, and a reopening of the future in trust as each accepts both the good and bad parts of the self and the other. . . . [Thus] the capacity to forgive another's offenses is directly related to the ability to deal with one's inner offender. As a person learns to deal with the bad objects within, bad objects in others become less troublesome. The ability to deal with the internal is requisite for dealing with the external.[25]

A person who lacks this kind of emotional maturity would tend to split both the self and the other as he regresses to earlier stages of development (the paranoid and schizoid positions). Such splitting accounts for the well-known phenomenon in which he sees himself as "all good" and the other as "all bad," while the other carries the "unowned, unacceptable parts of the self. . . . As we see these traits in the face of the foe, projections though they are, they disappear in the self. Anxiety and guilt, aided by selective perception and recall, now diminish and disappear."[26] The other is perceived to be all-powerful (like the formerly all-powerful parent), and the self is perceived to be little and helpless (like the infant he used to be and with whom he is unconsciously identified in this regressed state). Augsburger's observation at this point corroborates the conclusion already reached from a family systems perspective, namely, that "the degree to which one blames one's parents is the degree to which one is still stuck in the family of origin, is still a child."[27] Harsh though this judgment may sound to those adults unable to forgive their parents for the wrong done them, it nevertheless points to the central impasse where people find themselves "stuck" in both an inner and an outer sense. They are unable genuinely to come to terms with the past in such a way that they can prevent repeating it in another form. If they are psychologically still children blaming their parents, they will inevitably repeat the past in some form. Child psychotherapist Dorothy Martyn captures the essence of the problem: "Psychological distress in itself is not erasable because there is no way to start over. We are caught in an infinite series of mirrors in which repetition of man's error is inevitable because internalization from one's relational matrix is axiomatic."[28]

25. Augsburger, *Helping People Forgive,* 60-61, 64-65.

26. Augsburger, *Helping People Forgive,* 63.

27. Augsburger, *Helping People Forgive,* 63.

28. Dorothy Martyn, "A Child and Adam: A Parable of the Two Ages," *Journal of Religion and Health* 16 (1977): 278.

The normal psychological phenomenon of human functioning, psychic introjection, is thus responsible for the fact that the inner world and the outer world of our interpersonal relationships actually mirror each other. Thus our attitude toward the outer abuser is intimately entwined with our attitude toward "the inner abuser." The "inner abuser" would be the internalized representation of the person with whom we have a primary relationship in the outside world. He (or she) becomes an integral part of the self, with both good and bad characteristics. Growth or development in the outer relationship would inevitably have a powerful impact on our inner world; and coming to terms with the reality of the abuse inwardly could empower us to approach the parent in the external world. Inner and outer reality thus mirror one another. As Augsburger points out, "Our special relations [e.g., intimate relations with family] contain deep involvements, profound loyalties, intimate feelings, and covenantal obligations that connect us to inner layers of the soul, former selves in the developmental process, and other persons in our family systems. . . . We become systemically interrelated with the whole person and the other as a totality is connected with us."[29]

Because our parents live inside us as part of our own psychic constitution, cutting them off would be something like trying to excise a liver or heart, a part of our body essential for life. "Cutting off" parents as a way of managing anxiety and pain may provide temporary relief, but as an attempt at a permanent solution it is bound to have deleterious effects on everyone: on the perpetrator of the abuse, who never gets confronted with the effects of his sin; on the victim, who not only remains in a victimized position vis-à-vis her parents, but is also seriously split (i.e., cut off from herself) insofar as she avoids facing the internalized representations of her parents; and also on the whole extended family, who are adversely affected by the taboos and secrets related to the abuse, even if they themselves have no direct knowledge of it.[30]

Insofar as forgiveness and reconciliation are a psychological possibility, they involve processes of emotional maturing. From an interpersonal

29. Augsburger, *Helping People Forgive*, 34.

30. "Secrets function to divide a family, as an avalanche would a community. The most important effect of secrets on a family's emotional system is that they exacerbate other pathological processes unrelated to the content of the particular secret, because secrets generally function to keep anxiety at higher energy levels. [Secrets] are never on the side of challenge and change. Secrets are very serious stuff." Friedman, *Generation to Generation*, 52-54.

perspective, they require a person to be able to take a clear, differentiated stand. In terms of the concrete situation that we are considering, taking such a stand would be a matter of the victim taking her own suffering seriously enough to stand steadfastly with the emotionally traumatized child that she once was (and who therefore still lives inside her). It would involve a capacity to confront the abuser in some way with a description of the suffering she has undergone as a result of the abuse. It would include the recognition that what was done to her was unjust and intolerable. Taking steps toward some kind of reconciliation with the abuser therefore would not mean that she was offering him "cheap grace." On the contrary, she would confront him as a way of giving him the opportunity truly to repent the wrong he has committed. She would not be interested in hearing explanations that sought to deny his responsibility because of possible extenuating circumstances. In other words, even if the abuse arose out of the abuser's own terrible inheritance of twisted relationships, he nevertheless would need to take responsibility for his own actions. In recounting her suffering to the one who has harmed her, she would be giving the perpetrator an opportunity to begin genuinely to make amends. Far from being retaliatory or vindictive, confrontation in this sense could be one of the most loving and generous actions a victim could undertake.

From an intrapsychic perspective, emotional maturity would mean that the victim has come to terms with the fact that the abuser is also a part of her own psychic structure; that is to say, he is not only an outer person, but also a part of herself.

> We must face the truth that we are not merely innocent victims who have suffered at the hands of our families. Instead, we ourselves continue to wound others until we can become conscious of the hurt and anger within us and slowly let go of it. In working with clients who have been abused as children, it is always a sobering moment of truth when the one who was abused can finally see the ways he or she now abuses others. It is a scary but potentially liberating thing to see how the cycle we are trying so hard to escape is repeated with frighteningly unconscious accuracy in our own lives.[31]

What Bennett refers to here as "a sobering moment of truth" is that point in the therapeutic process when the victim realizes that she too is caught

---

31. Bennett, "Family Complexes and Individuation," 12.

in the same web of sin that already caught the parent who abused her. She, herself, is subject to the same powerful forces of hatred and rage, of defensiveness, self-righteousness, and self-deception that all flesh is heir to. But what makes the recognition of her own sin uncanny is its particular manifestation that has this "frighteningly unconscious accuracy." Eventually she comes to see that the abuser is also an internalized aspect of herself. She, herself, is a culpable sinner, unable by her own power to extract herself from the web in which she is caught.

If human beings are in truth knit together in sin and in grace, as the gospel attests ("But God shows his love for us in that while we were yet sinners Christ died for us" [Rom. 5:8]), it would seem that the only way out of the dilemma is somehow through the narrow gate of repentance and the renewal of life. This narrow gate is approached in the therapeutic process when a victim of abuse begins to catch glimpses of her own failings and sinfulness before God. But such glimpses would come only after the person has gone through a process of profound grief over the multiple losses involved in the abusive situation. "Adult reparations and adult mourning are possible when the objects within (both good and bad internalized identifications) are accepted; then others who act evilly (external bad objects) can be seen with empathy and compassion."[32] Abused persons who begin to mature emotionally in the ways described do so only by another relationship, a relationship in which they are listened to, believed, and understood, cared for and respected. In the context of a loving relationship with another who respects and safeguards proper human boundaries, they can begin to explore the pain and terror of what they have undergone.

The work of psychotherapy has long been conceptualized as a unique kind of "reparenting" process. Through the offering of a new relationship that symbolically recapitulates the relationship between parent and child, the therapist is internalized as a beneficent other, which eventually has a marked impact on the originally internalized parental representations.[33] The "good enough" therapist restores trust by respecting the person's inviolable personal boundaries and by providing a safe space in which she can grieve the immense losses of her childhood years. For if therapy is to bring healing, it will involve remembering the abuse, recalling concrete events and connecting them with the feelings she would have had, had she not dissociated herself from them. These feelings inevitably are the emotions

---

32. Augsburger, *Helping People Forgive,* 166.
33. Martyn, "A Child and Adam," 275-87.

inherent to the grieving process: shock, horror, fear, rage, outrage, sorrow, and despair, interspersed with recurring bouts of denial, minimization, bargaining, and numbness, when the intensity of raw feeling seems too overwhelming.[34] Sometimes improvement comes by allowing the emotions to emerge, even if no conscious memories can be attached to them. Put in its simplest form, emotional healing *is* grieving.

Once Gizelle broke through to her memories of the abuse, she was flooded with feelings that needed some kind of containment. Therapy by itself was no longer enough. She needed a whole community of persons to support and uphold her while she poured out the torrent of formerly repressed feelings that now threatened to overwhelm her.

> By that time, I had made a few good friends who stood by me. I started with a very sparse network of support, which has since spiraled, one person at a time. I felt so blessed with the support I had. I went home and made a list of all my dearest friends, female and male, and I said, "This is what I'm discovering. And I need someone to listen. I'm calling all my friends. I'm going to structure seven days, and I want you to tell me what day you can come, and if you can give me a commitment to come every Monday between two and four, it'd be great." And people came through. I talked and I talked. About my feelings. About the molestation. About my health. About my suicides. About my father. Giving it form. Giving it shape. Naming it. Feeling it. I just needed to have someone listen to me.[35]

But what about forgiveness? Was it possible in the context of this grief work for Gizelle to forgive her father? Regrettably, we are not told, for her story was still unfolding even as she related it to the authors of the volume in which it appeared. She had made great strides, however, in accepting the full range of her emotional responses, her rage and outrage toward her father, right alongside her feelings of love and compassion, thus showing that she had achieved the "depressive position." In her inner world, she was

---

34. Elisabeth Kübler-Ross first described the emotional stages of the grieving process in her celebrated book, *On Death and Dying,* as denial, anger, bargaining, depression, and acceptance. Since its publication, a general consensus has evolved that these are not stages that one follows in strict time sequence, but fluid steps that one can cycle through numerous times as one grieves a loss. Elisabeth Kübler-Ross, *On Death and Dying* (New York: Simon and Schuster, 1969).

35. Bass and Davis, *The Courage to Heal,* 454.

able to bring together the bad and the good of the self, and to recognize how her own struggles had in turn harmed her daughter, to whom she then sought to make amends. She was able, in other words, not only to attain a united self but also to begin to make amends for the trauma she inflicted on her daughter when she had despaired of life itself. At the same time, she was also able to acknowledge both the good and the bad in her father, no longer needing to see him only as evil. She recognized, for instance, something of his own suffering by acknowledging the dehumanizing hell from which he had come.

"It was soon after I was born that my father went away to Burma and spent two years in a MASH unit in the jungle, putting together blown-up bodies," Gizelle said. "When he came back, he was unable to work. He was in a lot of emotional difficulty. One of his best friends had committed suicide right after the war."[36] Acknowledgment of his suffering, however, did not excuse his actions, even if, from a Christian perspective, it set them into the proper context of the universality of sin, showing that his culpability was not his alone, but belonged in the larger context of the ravages and terrors of war and destruction of which human beings are frighteningly capable. Human sin is a mysterious combination of both guilt and power, at once a vast web in which we are caught and particular actions that we culpably undertake by our choices that keep us even more forcefully caught in sin's grip.

Gizelle was able to stand courageously with the abused child who was once herself (and who thus still lived in her), and tell her father that she remembered the incident in which he raped her. When he proceeded to deny it with some vehemence, she was not dissuaded from continuing her work, even though she did let go of the fantasy that he might help her or that some kind of reconciliation with him might be possible. She also made the brave decision not to protect her father by keeping the abuse a secret from her daughter. "And then I thought, 'No, that's where this is passed on. This is the denial that allows this to happen. My daughter has a right to know the truth of what's going on.'"[37] Near the end of her story she writes: "Sometimes I sit here and feel such compassion for my father, I weep. Other times I see myself taking a gun and shooting [him]. I am letting it all come right on through. And the more I allow all of it to come up, the more I find myself moving toward love. The more I block the rage,

36. Bass and Davis, *The Courage to Heal*, 447.
37. Bass and Davis, *The Courage to Heal*, 456.

the more I stay stuck. And so for me they're both right there. I reconcile it by saying I trust the process. I trust the validity of my outrage. The outrage is because I honor and value and love life."[38]

Although Gizelle herself did not undergo her therapeutic process as a Christian, it might be instructive for our own purposes to make some observations from an explicitly theological frame of reference. First, it is possible to interpret the work of a secular therapist as a sign of God's grace. The healing compassion and gifted insight of the therapist and the support of Gizelle's caring circle of friends can be seen as a sign of God's mercy that comes to Gizelle as a gift of grace and can be understood as a kind of secular parable of the truth.[39] For God's grace and mercy are not limited to working within the sphere of the church alone. The wind of God's healing Spirit blows where it will.

Second, there is an important distinction between the vertical and the horizontal dimensions of forgiveness. The so-called vertical dimension of God's forgiveness is based on God's free decision to be for us despite our wickedness toward others and godlessness toward him. "Because of Jesus Christ, God no longer holds my sins against me. Christ alone is my righteousness and my life; Christ is my only hope. Grace alone, not my merits, is the basis on which God has forgiven me in him."[40] The actuality of God's grace toward sinners not only assures us of our own forgiveness, but is also the condition for the possibility of our forgiving anyone who has harmed us. Only insofar as forgiveness is first received as God's unimaginable gift can it be offered to another in love. That is to say, only as we receive the actuality of God's forgiveness do we have the capacity to forgive another who has harmed us. Question 83 in the new Presbyterian catechism puts these vertical and horizontal dimensions of forgiveness into proper relationship. "How can you forgive those who have really hurt you?" it asks. "I cannot love my enemies, I cannot pray for those who persecute me, I cannot even be ready to forgive those who have really hurt me, without the grace that comes from above. I cannot be conformed to the image of God's Son, apart from the power of God's Word and Spirit. Yet I am promised that I can do all things through Christ who strengthens me."[41]

Third, it is a profound mistake to understand forgiveness as a law or

38. Bass and Davis, *The Courage to Heal*, 456.
39. Martyn, "A Child and Adam," 285.
40. *The Study Catechism* (Louisville: Westminster John Knox, 1998), question 80.
41. *The Study Catechism*, question 83.

moral demand rather than the gospel of life that it is. Alice Miller, the Swiss psychologist whose vocation has been to challenge the abusive child-rearing practices of her culture, shows how making forgiveness into a demand can itself be a form of moral violence. The demand to forgive another in this sense would function as a way of adding layers of guilt and shame to an already overburdened and traumatized soul. The abused person thus wonders why she is unable to forgive and further injures herself by heaping guilt upon herself for being selfish and unforgiving. Miller rejects reconciliation as a goal of the therapeutic process. She writes: "Since, to me, therapy means a sensory, emotional and mental discovery of the long-repressed truth, I regard the moral demand for reconciliation with parents as an inevitable blocking and paralyzing of the therapeutic process."[42] How would the "moral demand for reconciliation" block and paralyze the work of healing? It would prevent the person from recalling her own experiences and feeling her own emotions. By putting an overlay of a "should" over her feelings, it would effectively alienate her from herself. And that is the thing that very likely happened to Gizelle as a child. A child with abusive parents is typically instructed as to how she "should" act, how she "should" feel, indeed, how she "should" completely forgo her own true feelings and put forth an acceptable, but false, front. Telling her in the context of therapeutic work that she "should" forgive her parents would only perpetuate this destructive pattern.

The authors of the book in which Gizelle's story appears do not wish to jeopardize the healing process of survivors of abuse by any such moral demands for forgiveness or reconciliation. In their chapter on forgiveness they write:

> The only necessity as far as healing is concerned is forgiving yourself. Developing compassion and forgiveness for your abuser, or for the members of your family who did not protect you, is not a required part of the healing process. It is not something to hope for or shoot for. It is not the final goal. . . . You may never reach an attitude of forgiveness, and that's perfectly all right. . . . "Why should you [forgive]? First they steal everything else from you and then they want forgiveness too? Let them get their own. You've given enough."[43]

42. Alice Miller, *Banished Knowledge: Facing Childhood Injuries* (New York: Doubleday, 1990), 154.

43. Bass and Davis, *The Courage to Heal,* 149-50.

While the bitterness of such an attitude is an understandable human reaction, can we say from a Christian perspective that it is even possible to grant ourselves such forgiveness? As mere creatures and not God, are we able to grant ourselves forgiveness any more than we can create ourselves or grant ourselves eternal life? Are we not dependent upon our fellow human beings and on God himself to grant us the forgiveness of our sins? There is nothing in the New Testament about forgiving ourselves, although there is much there to indicate a close connection between our forgiveness of another and God's forgiveness of us. ("Forgive us our debts, as we forgive our debtors." "What you bind on earth is bound in heaven and what you loose on earth is loosed in heaven.")[44] If forgiveness is not law, but rather gospel, then it is not properly understood as a therapeutic goal, or even as something we should strive willfully to attain, but only as something we can pray for. While we cannot forgive another as an act of the will, we can by grace willingly pray for the capacity to forgive one who has harmed us.

But this perspective also raises the question of our fourth point: the relationship between healing and forgiveness. The authors here seem to indicate that forgiveness of the abuser is not a necessary element for emotional healing to occur. While it may be helpful to forgive oneself, so they seem to say, there is no necessity to forgive one's abuser in order to heal. One can heal without taking the abuser into consideration at all. Forgiveness is thus seen only from a perspective of its instrumental value for healing. From the perspective of Christian theology, however, forgiveness could never be such an instrumental value, for it is an end in itself. Forgiveness is God's unfathomable gift of grace to humanity, a gift that enables us to be set free from the power of guilt and sin to destroy us. Emotional healing, from this perspective, would be understood within the context of forgiveness, rather than the other way around. Healing in this view would be considered a sign of God's mercy and grace that points beyond itself to the salvation accomplished apart from us in Jesus Christ. That is to say, emotional healing would be understood as a kind of inbreaking of the kingdom, a little light that would encourage hope for the greater light of salvation promised to break forth at the end of all things. The theological significance of healing

44. L. Gregory Jones also addresses this problem in what he calls "therapeutic forgiveness." He says that "forgiveness, at least as Christians ought to understand and embody it, is not about 'healing ourselves,' it is about being healed by God and by others in and through specific practices of forgiveness." L. Gregory Jones, *Embodying Forgiveness: A Theological Analysis* (Grand Rapids: Eerdmans, 1995), 50.

for the believer is its function as a sign of our eschatological hope for all persons. Conceptually, healing and forgiveness thus stand in a particular relation to each other. "They occur on two different levels and indicate two different contexts of meaning. Whereas the significance of the one is temporal, the significance of the other is eternal; whereas the one is penultimate, the other is ultimate. . . . The significance of salvation as the ultimate term is thus independent of that of healing as the penultimate term, but the relationship is irreversible, for the significance of the penultimate depends on that of the ultimate."[45] While healing of a sort can occur without forgiveness, the ultimate unity of the two is "eschatological in form," namely, in the final salvation of the world in Jesus Christ. All our attempts at human healing and human forgiveness are inevitably fragmentary and partial. When forgiveness occurs as an actual human event, however, it feels indeed like a miracle and cannot help but bring in its train a tremendous release of joy and deeper emotional healing. For Christians, it points beyond itself as a joyful sign of God's coming kingdom when God will be all in all.

Fifth, there is an important distinction between forgiveness and reconciliation. Some have argued that in situations of abuse, Christians should not forgive the perpetrator unless and until there is evidence of genuine repentance. Thus, Marie Fortune argues that confession, repentance, and restitution are all necessary actions to be taken by the perpetrator before a victim of abuse should forgive. "Prior to justice," she writes, "forgiveness is an empty exercise." She goes on to say, "Forgiveness before justice is 'cheap grace' and cannot contribute to authentic healing and restoration to wholeness for the victim or for the offender. It cuts the healing process short and may well perpetuate the cycle of abuse. It also undercuts the redemption of abusers by preventing them from being accountable for their abusive behavior."[46] It is understandable that Fortune would argue against the dangers of premature forgiveness, particularly since it is known that perpetrators of abuse have little awareness of the costliness of the forgiveness they ask for. Offenders might seem remorseful after battering their partners and terrifying their children, and might offer what seems like a sincere apology. Yet within days or weeks, the cycle begins again with a

---

45. Deborah van Deusen Hunsinger, *Theology and Pastoral Counseling: A New Interdisciplinary Approach* (Grand Rapids: Eerdmans, 1995), 74-75.

46. Marie Fortune, *Violence in the Family: A Workshop Curriculum for Clergy and Other Helpers,* rev. ed. (Cleveland: Pilgrim Press, 1991), 174.

buildup of tension leading to another explosion of anger and family members being badly hurt. Insisting on a repentance in which the perpetrator gives evidence of starting anew by actually taking steps to change his ways seems to be the better part of wisdom. Not mere good intentions are called for, but rather actions that show genuine remorse and a commitment to change. Withholding forgiveness is thus set forth as a kind of strategy to demonstrate that change has to happen before anything can be forgiven. One group of incest offenders who were in a treatment program actually spoke out against forgiveness because it gave them the message that they were not going to be held accountable for their actions. "A group of incest offenders in a treatment program made a powerful plea: 'Don't forgive so easily.' All were Christians and had gone to their pastors as soon as they were arrested, asking to be forgiven. Each had been prayed over, forgiven and sent home. They said that this pastoral response had been the least helpful to them because it enabled them to continue to avoid accountability for their offenses."[47] It is truly horrifying to think of someone continuing in sin because a priest or minister had forgiven him. Somewhere the preaching of the church has failed. What kind of distortions of the gospel are we perpetrating because we no longer know how to hold people accountable, because we have eliminated all forms of church discipline? "What shall we say then? Are we to continue in sin that grace may abound? By no means! How can we who died to sin still live in it?" (Rom. 6:1-2).

And yet, it seems more true to the gospel to say that while there can be no real reconciliation without repentance, there could indeed be occasions of forgiveness without repentance. That is to say, though reconciliation depends upon genuine repentance, forgiveness itself hinges neither upon healing nor upon repentance. Just as forgiveness is not an instrumental value for healing, so it cannot function as a strategic ploy to keep offenders in line. Forgiveness is God's free gift freely offered. If "Christ died for us while we were yet sinners," the forgiveness extended to us was not conditional. One might argue, in fact, that it is the free offering of this unconditional grace that actually enables us to see the depth of our own sin against God. In the light of God's gracious forgiveness, in other words, our sin is all the more starkly revealed. The victim of abuse does not need to wait for the offender to repent before forgiving him.[48] Forgiveness sets

47. Fortune, *Violence in the Family,* 178.

48. Margaret R. Holmgren argues on philosophical grounds (from a standpoint in virtue-ethics), that because offenders (like victims) are "sentient beings and moral agents," they

the forgiver free from bitterness and dark desires for revenge. Forgiveness also sets the offender free from unbearable burdens of guilt, regret, shame, and remorse, free to begin anew a life lived in Christ. While it is possible that Gizelle's forgiveness of her father may one day lead him to repent of his violence and brutality toward her, he might also remain in denial, never to acknowledge the truth of what actually occurred between them. In such a case, reconciliation would be an impossibility. Reconciliation would require her father openly to acknowledge the truth, take genuine responsibility for his actions, express sincere sorrow, and take concrete steps that communicate how seriously and earnestly he desires his daughter's renewed trust. True reconciliation would thus in the mystery of God's grace actually transform the relationship between them even though it wouldn't erase the pain and anguish of the past.[49]

Sixth, how might Gizelle's therapeutic process have been different if the church and its practices had been the overarching context for her work of healing? Would it have made a difference if Gizelle had sought out a Christian pastoral counselor for her therapeutic work, that is, if she herself had sought healing as a Christian disciple? If it made a difference, what sort of difference would that be?

Pastoral counseling, at least as practiced in the United States today, would perhaps not look very different from the kind of therapy Gizelle received. Lamentably, the pastoral counseling movement has in large part forsaken the traditions and doctrinal riches of the church in its work. But if the pastoral counseling sought were Christian, it would not only avail itself of the treasury of psychoanalytic insight, but would also self-

---

need to be treated with "an attitude of respect, compassion, and real goodwill" (p. 98), which is her *definition* of forgiveness. In this case, forgiveness needs to be offered unconditionally, even without any repentance on the part of the offender. She helpfully outlines six steps that are intrinsic to the victim's self-respect and to her healing: (1) recover her self-esteem; (2) differentiate between forgiving and condoning the wrong done to her; (3) acknowledge her true (often intense) feelings about the incident; (4) take steps to protect herself from further victimization; (5) if she feels the need to express her feelings directly to the offender, to do so with the support of others; (6) determine whether she wants to seek restitution from the offender. See Margaret R. Holmgren, *Forgiveness and Retribution: Responding to Wrongdoing* (New York: Cambridge University Press, 2012), 58-64.

49. For a helpful discussion of the dangers of "premature forgiveness," the relationship between forgiveness and reconciliation, and what it means for the church to be called to be "ambassadors of reconciliation," see Pamela Cooper-White's concluding chapter in *The Cry of Tamar: Violence against Women and the Church's Response* (Minneapolis: Fortress, 2012), 251-61.

consciously draw from the wealth to be found in the Scripture, prayer, doctrine, preaching, worship, sacraments, and fellowship of the church. While Gizelle herself did not seek Christian pastoral counseling, it could be instructive to imagine what it might have looked like if she had. Three brief observations may be in order.

First, the work of healing would not be the work of an isolated individual, nor even of an individual with her therapist and her friends. While it is impressive to see Gizelle's creativity at work as she sought to gather a group of friends to help her heal from the trauma of her past, there is for me considerable pathos in pondering how hard she had to work to create a community of care for herself. How meager and threadbare it seems by comparison to the church as a living community, given as a gift from God. There is something poignant about Gizelle calling friends and asking for individual commitments of two-hour time slots. Each friend is connected to Gizelle like a spoke on a wheel with Gizelle at the center, but no one spoke is intrinsically connected to any other spoke. The friends may not even know each other. The Monday afternoon listener has likely never met the Monday evening friend. So many of our contemporary efforts to create "communities of care" strike me as just such patchwork affairs pieced together by huge expenditures of individual initiative, rather than a rich interwoven tapestry where everyone is connected to everyone else by each person's connection to Jesus Christ. Gizelle's crying need, as her actions so vividly demonstrate, is for a whole community to surround her with love and care. That need is not Gizelle's alone, but every person's in our atomized and rootless society.

Second, how might the church become a real agent of reconciliation, where it could actually provide safe and structured settings for parents and their adult children to meet face-to-face? How can forgiveness actually take place under current conditions of modern life if parents and children never come together to talk about their common painful history? Estranged families sustained by the daily bread of Scripture could develop an imagination for human forgiveness (as in the story of Joseph and his brothers), could take heed from cautionary tales of warning (like Tamar and Amnon and Absalom), and could visualize anew goals worth striving for (like "speaking the truth in love"). The intercessory prayers of the community could uphold all those who cannot bring themselves even to ask for the willingness to forgive.

Finally, when faced with the magnitude of the hurt, it seems obvious that a psychotherapist or pastoral counselor, no matter how gifted, would simply be incapable of providing the level of care needed to restore a single individual to renewed life. Yet that seems to be what many of us have been trying to do in many of our contemporary therapeutic practices. It is significant that Anna Freud saw the clear limits of psychotherapy more than fifty years ago. Robert Coles recounts a conversation he once had with Miss Freud, in which she described the painful psychiatric history of an elderly woman. Then she wondered aloud what they (as psychotherapists, as human beings) would really desire for her. "Oh, I don't mean psychotherapy!" she exclaimed.

> She's had lots of that. It would take more years, I suspect, of psychoanalysis than the good Lord has given her. . . . I will confess to you: when I was listening to all of this, I thought to myself that this poor old lady doesn't need us at all. No she's had her fill of "us," even if she doesn't know it. . . . What she needs . . . is forgiveness. She needs to make peace with her soul, not talk about her mind. There must be a God, somewhere, to help her, to hear her, to heal her. . . . But I fear she'll not find him! And we certainly aren't the ones who will be of assistance to her in that regard![50]

But who are the ones who will be of assistance in that regard if not Christian pastors and pastoral counselors? Can Christian pastoral counselors once again claim the full power of the gospel as intrinsic to the vocation to which they are called?

---

50. Robert Coles, *Harvard Diary: Reflections on the Sacred and the Secular* (New York: Crossroad, 1990), 177-80, cited in Johann Christoph Arnold, *Seventy Times Seven: The Power of Forgiveness* (Farmington, Pa.: Plough Publishing House, 1997), 133-34.

CHAPTER 4

Keeping an Open Heart in Troubled Times

Self-Empathy as a Christian Spiritual Practice

How do you keep your heart open when you see person after person afflicted with trauma? I used to think that 95 percent of the female population in this country had been sexually abused as children.[1] Were the statistics of sexual abuse vastly underreported, I wondered, or was my perception skewed because of my work as a pastoral counselor? When you listen to stories of pain day after day, how do you keep your own spirit alive? The root meaning of the word "compassion" is "to suffer with." What do you do when you reach the limit of your capacity for compassion?

We are contextual beings whose many contexts exist not simply outside us but also within us. As one member of a particular family, we internalize every member in it, along with the family culture as a whole with its unique dynamics, both for good and for ill. Similarly, as cultural beings, we dwell within a particular culture, but that culture also dwells in us.[2] We internalize the context in which we live, a context so complex that it would take hours adequately to describe it.[3]

---

1. See Pamela Cooper-White's chapter "The Sexual Abuse of Children," in *The Cry of Tamar: Violence against Women and the Church's Response* (Minneapolis: Fortress, 2012), 168-92. See also Nancy J. Ramsay, "Sexual Abuse and Shame: The Travail of Recovery," in *Women in Travail and Transition: A New Pastoral Care,* ed. Jeanne Stevenson-Moessner and Maxine Glaz (Minneapolis: Fortress, 1991), 109-25.

2. A. J. van den Blink, "Empathy amid Diversity: Problems and Possibilities," *Journal of Pastoral Theology* (Summer 1993): 8.

3. For a fascinating firsthand account of some of the cultural, socioeconomic, and theological factors that influenced her own beliefs about self-care, see Teresa E. Snorton, "Self-Care for the African American Woman," in *In Her Own Time: Women and Developmental Issues in Pastoral Care,* ed. Jeanne Stevenson-Moessner (Minneapolis: Fortress, 2000), 285-94.

The overarching context that each of us has internalized — that affects us daily, body and soul — includes the tragic events of September 11, 2001, the wars in Iraq and Afghanistan, and the daily terror and anguish of those in the Middle East. Depending on which issues live in our hearts, we may also bear the pain of those who suffer from HIV-AIDS, political oppression, torture, or any number of tragic features of today's world. As members of a common humanity, each of us participates in the world's distress. Those of us in ministry internalize certain levels of pain by our commitment to be fully present with the handful of persons we serve on a daily basis. The cumulative effect of being in the presence of so much pain puts us in danger of compassion fatigue, in which we simply reach our limits.[4] We stop caring, not because we want to, but because we no longer have the capacity to take in anything more.

Philip Hallie, author of *Lest Innocent Blood Be Shed,* describes the danger of having a vocation that continually confronts one with suffering and evil. He writes of researching the Nazi era:

> For years, I had been studying the slow crushing and grinding of a human being by other human beings. . . . Across all these studies, the pattern of the strong crushing the weak kept repeating itself and repeating itself, so that when I was not bitterly angry, I was bored at the repetition of the patterns of persecution. When I was not desiring to be cruel with the cruel, I was a monster — like, perhaps, many others around me — who could look upon torture and death without a shudder.[5]

Being exposed to evil in this secondhand way had taken a heavy toll on Hallie's spirit, even without his knowing it. Harry Wilmer, a Jungian analyst who studied the repetitive nightmares of Vietnam veterans ten years after the war had ended, acknowledges something of the personal cost. "It goes almost without saying that my work with these men was often painful to me. Many times I asked myself why I had taken it on, or more correctly, why it had taken me on. At times I experienced war nightmares and dreams of combat. Then I knew that the suffering of the men was getting to me."[6] While Hallie apparently defended against the pain for a while, he came to see that he had

---

4. See B. Hudnall Stamm, *Professional Quality of Life: Compassion Satisfaction and Fatigue Subscales, R-IV (ProQOL).* www.proqol.org/ProQol_Test.html.

5. Philip Hallie, *Lest Innocent Blood Be Shed* (New York: Harper and Row, 1979), 2.

6. Harry A. Wilmer, "The Healing Nightmare: A Study of the War Dreams of Vietnam Combat Veterans," *Quadrant* 19, no. 1 (Spring 1986): 57.

done so at the cost of his own humanity. Wilmer, by contrast, allowed the veterans' suffering to affect him intimately. Years after the war had ended, he himself awoke at night in a sweat of terror. The war lived on, as he says, "in the nightmares of combat veterans and in the collective unconscious of us all."[7]

In January 2006 my husband, George Hunsinger, organized a national conference for religious and military leaders, human rights activists, and lawyers to launch the National Religious Campaign against Torture, a group of "national, regional, and local religious and secular organizations committed to ensuring that the United States does not engage in torture or cruel, inhuman and degrading treatment of anyone, without exceptions."[8] My husband spends hours each day reading volumes of material on the Internet about our current world crisis. Books on torture are piled on the breakfast table, in the living room, and on the floor beside the bed. Stories of torture fill his heart, fueling his commitment to do what he can to bring these horrifying practices to an end.

One evening some time ago, as I went to him to say goodnight, he began to tell me about what he was reading. Worried about the next day's responsibilities, I interrupted him, stating emphatically that I couldn't bear to hear stories about torture right before going to bed. I was anxious about lying awake for hours seeing these images over and over in my mind's eye. No longer able to keep my heart open, I told my husband with considerable energy that *I just could not bear* to hear one more story of trauma.

As I have reflected on that moment, I have come to see something of the cost of telling myself that "I cannot bear it." First, I cut myself off from the solace of shared suffering, in this case my husband's and my own. In subsequent weeks, my husband acknowledged that he was now consciously keeping such stories from me. Second, I found that I was shielding myself from any news that might upset my peace of mind or interfere with my ability to concentrate. Third, I felt regret over constricting my awareness in this way, limiting my freedom to learn and to act. The victims of torture were actually suffering torture while I could not even bear to hear about it. Wanting to *expand* my capacities for compassion rather than shrink away from such stories in self-protection, I found myself at odds with my core values.

This, then, is the dilemma: How do I keep an open heart toward those who need my compassion, whether it is my husband with whom I share my life, myself, as I face my very real limits, or the victims of torture living

7. Wilmer, "The Healing Nightmare," 47.
8. http://www.nrcat.org/, accessed August 26, 2009.

in prisons or dungeons whose very lives may depend upon the willingness of others to feel their plight and act on their behalf?

Nonviolent Communication: Self-Empathy

In his book *Nonviolent Communication: A Language of Life,* Marshall Rosenberg teaches a mode of consciousness and a set of skills that enable us not only to practice empathic reception of others, but also to learn how to respond empathically to ourselves.[9] While empathy is considered an essential skill for pastoral care, I do not believe that it can flourish apart from self-empathy. To hear another with compassion, we need first to hear ourselves with compassion. If our anxiety is triggered (as mine was when my husband wished to share a story of torture), we are unable to hear little beyond our own internal static. As I have written elsewhere, "Much of the self-discipline required in listening to others without interjecting one's own reactions develops as one learns to pay attention to one's anxiety. In order to focus on another, one must know, paradoxically, how to pay attention to oneself."[10]

In nonviolent communication, Rosenberg teaches us how to pay attention not only to our feelings but also to the underlying needs or values that are causing the feelings. Needs are understood to be universal qualities that enhance life. They are life-giving, by definition. Thus, all human beings have physical needs, such as food, rest, water, warmth, and shelter. But just as essential to human thriving are our interpersonal needs for love, acceptance, understanding, community, and mutuality, among others. In addition, we might identify spiritual needs for forgiveness, hope, courage, trust, faith, integrity. These brief lists are meant to be suggestive, not definitive. What is pertinent here is that needs are evidence of our basic humanity. Though they transcend culture, each culture has its own particular way of understanding and expressing them. For Rosenberg, human needs are the underlying motivation for all our choices, whether we are conscious of them or not.[11] When our needs are met, we typically feel satisfied, delighted, or joyful. When our needs are unmet, we might feel frustrated, angry, sorrowful, or perplexed.

9. Marshall Rosenberg, *Nonviolent Communication: A Language of Life* (Encinitas, Calif.: PuddleDancer Press, 2003), chap. 9.

10. Deborah van Deusen Hunsinger, *Pray without Ceasing: Revitalizing Pastoral Care* (Grand Rapids: Eerdmans, 2006), 85.

11. Rosenberg, *Nonviolent Communication,* chap. 5.

When we have chronically unmet needs, we experience emotional pain and need healing. When we attune ourselves inwardly with an attitude of caring attentiveness toward ourselves, seeking to understand our own feelings and needs, we are practicing self-empathy. I believe that we cannot remain openhearted toward others unless we know how to metabolize our own pain. In the example above, I was unable to connect with my husband's pain because I was not fully present to my own. I needed more understanding of my reaction to his request to share what he was reading. Why, I wondered, did I interrupt him with such intensity?

I have come to regard moments like these, when I am "triggered" into uncharacteristic reactivity, as significant nodal points of potential healing and growth. I believe that any time I react rather than respond, it is because forces outside my awareness are at work. This is the "psychopathology of everyday life" that Freud describes so lucidly. Slips of the tongue, moments of lightning rage, and irritability over which I have no apparent control are opportunities to become aware of unknown forces at work within me. In nonviolent communication (NVC) terms, they are opportunities to practice self-empathy in order to connect with unmet needs.

The life-giving human needs at work in me were as yet impossible for me to grasp. On the surface, my need for rest seemed paramount. Yet the intensity of my reaction signaled that something deeper was possibly at stake. In the days and weeks that followed, I found myself repeating the words "I cannot bear it." I would say to myself, "I cannot bear to hear the stories of abused and tortured human beings; I simply cannot bear it." Though I understood this kind of self-talk to be life-alienating, something that disconnected me from myself and others, I did not know how to change it.

Practicing Self-Empathy

Self-empathy gives us the opportunity to listen to our own hearts with the same quality of compassionate attention that we would offer another in our best moments. However, simply *finding words* that accurately describe our feelings and needs is not the same as actually *connecting with them*. The process of connecting with an activated need in any particular situation requires us first to notice what is happening in the body. We ask ourselves gently what it is that we are seeking: "What is the longing of our heart?" As we listen for the answer, we focus on what goes on in our body, not on words in our mind.

As we attend to the body, we are seeking to name the unmet need that activated the feeling of frustration or pain. NVC teaches a kind of exquisite awareness of the range and variety of human needs. When several needs are tied up together in a gnarled ball, it takes time, care, and patience to identify each one. When we discover and accurately connect with the activated need(s), we experience an internal shift in the body. By internal shift, I mean something similar to what we experience when we finally remember a person's name that has been on "the tip of our tongue." When we discover the name, our body relaxes; we might give a deep sigh and say, "Ahh, I am so *relieved* to have remembered her name." In NVC, a similar feeling of shift and relaxation comes when we find the need that matches our feeling.[12]

So, for example, when I am upset by the kitchen piled high with dirty dishes, I want to identify my underlying need. Is it, I wonder, a need for order? Am I upset because I value a sense of order and beauty in my surroundings? Or is my underlying need one for trust and reliability? Perhaps I had a conversation with a family member who promised to clean the kitchen before going off with friends but did not follow through on that promise. Or is it really support that I need most of all? Are guests coming in thirty minutes and I am desperately needing support to make everything ready? The need, in other words, is always nested in a set of particular circumstances. I alone can identify my true need by attuning myself to how my body responds. What need, if met, would bring about palpable relaxation in my body?

The feelings I identify then become the thread that takes me deeper into my underlying longings. The feelings are usually more on the surface, whereas the needs are the buried treasure. We can feel the same feelings for weeks, months, even decades; they remain inert, a simple story that we tell again and again unless we connect with the unfulfilled desires that are causing the feelings. In NVC it is not necessary to understand the problem intellectually to bring about clarity or release. In fact, intellectual understanding can actually delay or block the desired liberating shift.

In order fully to connect with my need (rather than merely identifying *the word*), I might imagine a situation where that need is fully met. For example, I *connect emotionally* with the joy I feel whenever I see this quality in myself or anyone else (e.g., order, trust, reliability, or support, to take the example

---

12. Readers familiar with Eugene Gendlin's *focusing* will see close parallels with the practices he teaches. Both Rosenberg and Gendlin were students of Carl Rogers. See Eugene Gendlin, *Focusing* (New York: Bantam Books, 1982).

above). In other words, truly to connect with the need means that I imagine it as something fulfilled and present rather than as something lacking.

Truly to connect with the need is to experience its life-giving power. When I check how it feels in my body not to have the need met, I notice a heavy, tight, or constricted feeling. To connect with its *life-giving value,* by contrast, I shift to imagine the need being fully met. How do I actually feel *in my body* when I have order and beauty surrounding me, for example, or when I trust that those I live with will follow through on their promises? When I identify the actual need at work in the specific circumstances, I will experience a shift *in my body* when I ask myself this question. As I look inwardly with self-empathy, I am looking for an inner sense of release or relaxation, an *"aha"* feeling: *this* is the quality of being that I want in my life. "I want my surroundings to be orderly and beautiful because that gives me peace and joy." I don't focus, in other words, on the dirty dishes or the messy kitchen, but rather on the feeling in my body when the need is met.

Connecting with the need means to connect with its beauty, as one NVC trainer has put it.[13] It means that we live in a consciousness of this need or quality as an enduring value in our life. When we dwell in the need, we celebrate its presence and mourn its absence. When we feel the pain associated with its absence, we shift our attention to the joy of its intrinsic beauty or preciousness. Connected inwardly to its life-giving goodness, we may consent to living vulnerably with our unfulfilled longings.

Self-Empathy as Opening the Heart

In an NVC workshop on self-empathy, NVC trainer Robert Gonzales asked us to identify a sentence in our minds that seemed to disconnect us from ourselves or others. I knew that the sentence "I cannot bear it" truly disconnected me from others because I had seen how it had disconnected me from my husband. I was also aware that it alienated me from myself.

I began, with Robert's guidance, to repeat the phrase "I cannot bear it." Because we were working on "old" material (as opposed to a current trigger), Robert encouraged me to repeat the phrase several times until I could become fully connected to the emotions associated with it. After several repetitions, the underlying pain searing my soul emerged. What

---

13. I first learned of the "beauty of human needs" from Robert Gonzales, Ph.D., at an NVC International Intensive Training session in Rochester, N.Y., in July 2004.

was it *in particular* that I was telling myself I could not bear? What was the *specific observation* that I was reacting to?[14] In this case, the observation was not something my husband had actually said, but something I had remembered from an earlier conversation. What in particular I could not bear was the torture technique of waterboarding, in which human beings were brought to the very brink of drowning, and the hypothermia techniques that put naked prisoners into cold prison cells. Shivering and miserable, they were denied the most basic human need for warmth. As I lay snug in my bed at night with my down comforter wrapped around me, I would meditate on their plight until I thought I would go mad with the terror, the rage, and the sorrow of it.

As I began to tell Robert the specific images that haunted my imagination, my tears began to flow, to the point that my words were swallowed up by sobs. Robert did not simply hear my agony; he listened *for my needs.* He heard and reflected back each need with care. "You long for compassion for these prisoners. You want respect *for all people,* no matter what their sins or crimes. You want the truth to be spoken. You want it known what our country is doing to human beings in our name."

It required intense concentration as I struggled to give words to every facet of the pain. Then suddenly, unexpectedly, *when every need had been fully heard and named,* I became calm. I said matter-of-factly: "I can bear it because I just did. I can bear it because you were willing to hear it."[15]

Further Reflections

As I processed what had just occurred, I was astonished to realize that in shielding myself from the pain I felt, I had been perpetuating the very

14. In nonviolent communication, it is necessary to specify the exact thing one is reacting to so that there is clarity about the triggering issue. One aims to describe the specific observation (the precise words or events that were seen, heard, or remembered) in any communication with oneself or others. The NVC "template" for complete communication is OFNR: observation, feeling, need, request. See http://www.cnvc.org/en/online-learning/ nvc-concepts/nonviolent-communication, accessed August 26, 2009.

15. One of the reasons I felt so fully heard and received was the expression of anguish on Robert's face as he listened. I was moved by his willingness to enter into my suffering with such compassion. The example also shows the interconnection between empathy and self-empathy. I was unable to have empathy for myself until I had received empathy from another.

thing I abhorred. In a strange way, I was unwilling to acknowledge what we were doing to other human beings because I continually told myself that I could not bear to do so. I was unwilling to speak the truth as I understood it because I feared plunging others into the same nightmare of raw pain, fear, and grief that I was avoiding in myself. I, myself, thus kept the very complicity of silence that would enable these practices to continue. Were there others, I wondered, who also told themselves that they could not bear to acknowledge the truth? Did I now understand something of the horror and shame, I wondered, the sickening feeling, that might have swept the hearts of our German brothers and sisters during the Nazi era when they heard whispers of what was being done in their name?

Self-Empathy as a Christian Spiritual Practice

NVC is a form of consciousness and a set of skills that have an implicit spirituality all their own.[16] Depending on the theological assumptions of any particular teacher, different aspects will be emphasized. I have been instructed and edified over the years, as I have learned from serious practitioners of other religious paths how NVC has contributed to their ability to live out their deepest convictions. This ongoing interreligious dialogue is a fascinating subject that unfortunately lies outside the scope of this book. From the beginning of my own study of NVC, however, my interest has been in how it can be used practically in living out the gospel. My specific focus here is how I understand self-empathy as a Christian spiritual practice.

As a Christian, I am aware that my needs and core values are deeply shaped by the gospel. Whenever I seek to respond empathically to others, I am assuming that they, like all human beings, have, in the words of John Webster, "a given teleology. . . . They are not simply discrete units of personal need, but are what they are as they belong to an order of reality with certain ends."[17] I understand the order of reality to which they belong as the kingdom of God. In other words, I understand all human need in the

16. See, for example, http://www.cnvc.org/en/learn-online/spiritual-basis/spiritual-basis-nonviolent-communication, accessed August 26, 2009.

17. "Response" [to Caroline Simon] by John Webster, *For the Sake of the World: Karl Barth and the Future of Ecclesial Theology,* ed. George Hunsinger (Grand Rapids: Eerdmans, 2004), 163.

light of the prayer that Jesus taught, that God's kingdom should come, on earth as it is in heaven.

In my personal anguish over the plight of the tortured, I recognized my own most urgent need for the balm of human compassion. What I could not bear to imagine was the apparent lack of compassion for the suffering of human beings who were denied access to the most fundamental human need for breath and warmth. How could human beings so harden their hearts toward other human beings who, like them, were made in the image of God?

It is a curious fact that in the New Testament the verb for our word "compassion" is used only of Jesus or of the God figure in Jesus' parables.[18] I have come to see that my understanding of compassion has an inevitable christological shape. My faith has been decisively shaped by the stories of Jesus' compassion for the blind, the deaf, and the lame, for the ill and the grief-stricken. I am moved by the stories in which he has compassion on the crowds, in which he feeds the thousands who hunger for bread and for the smallest morsel of hope. I am astounded by his words of compassion toward those who brought about his death. In all these ways and more, I understand Jesus' compassion to be "a window of access into the nature of . . . God's vulnerability and willingness to suffer with us."[19] I believe that Robert's willingness to open his heart with compassion toward me had its source in God's grace, enabling him to "participate in God's compassion for the world."[20] Compassion, in my understanding, does not arise out of our own finally limited human capacities, but is grounded instead in *God's* love for the world.

Whenever I practice self-empathy, I am in search of what I most deeply need in any given situation. Though I can sometimes be badly mistaken in assessing my true need, in Christian worship, song, and prayer I confess my need of God and of God's grace in its rich multiplicity of forms. When discouraged, I need patience or courage. If I am disappointed in myself, I may identify my need as a sturdy sense of integrity or a more complete honesty. When afraid, I may recognize that I am lacking trust. If I only had more faith, I could act with more freedom. If I am in despair, I recognize my need for hope. Our human needs, in other words, are all ultimately

---

18. Andrew Purves, *The Search for Compassion: Spirituality and Ministry* (Louisville: Westminster John Knox, 1989), 16.

19. Purves, *The Search for Compassion*, 16.

20. Purves, *The Search for Compassion*, 12.

rooted and grounded in God. They are not finally qualities that we can develop on our own but are rather gifts that come from above.

It follows, therefore, that self-empathy as a Christian spiritual practice leads directly to prayer: to asking God for what I need. When I turn to God in prayer, I don't simply rattle off requests as if I were reading a grocery list. Instead, I meditate on the true nature of my need, and offer it up to God, trusting him as the author of every good and perfect gift. I cling to the promise that God will hear my requests and meet my needs (or else give me the strength to live in the midst of unmet need): "Rejoice in the Lord always. . . . The Lord is at hand. Have no anxiety about anything, but in everything by prayer and supplication with thanksgiving let your requests be made known to God" (Phil. 4:4-6). "And my God will supply every need of yours according to his riches in glory in Christ Jesus" (Phil. 4:19).

Prayer connects us to God and to all the needs that are fulfilled in him.[21] Through its stories and images of our core human needs fulfilled in the person of Jesus Christ, the gospel actually shapes the awareness of our needs. Jesus Christ is presented as the light of the world, fulfilling our human longings for illumination, for wisdom, for understanding; as the bread of life, fulfilling our daily need for basic sustenance, both body and soul; as the water of life, assuaging the thirst of every soul that aches for justice and peace. There is no longer any separation between *your* need and *my* need; there is simply *human* need that God alone can fulfill. Praying fervently about our needs deepens our sense of longing for God's kingdom to come on earth as it is in heaven. Indeed, it magnifies our longing until we join the groaning of creation for the new world to come (Rom. 8:22-23).

The gospel also underscores our fundamental need of one another. In the body of Christ, the church, we recognize our profound need for community, for mutual care, forgiveness, and love. "The eye cannot say to the hand, 'I have no need of you,' nor again the head to the feet, 'I have no need of you'" (1 Cor. 12:21). Our attempts to be self-sufficient are revealed as signs of our fallenness and sin. We need one another as fundamentally as a "fish needs water." Karl Barth comments: "My humanity depends upon the fact that I am always aware, and my action is determined by the awareness, that I need the assistance of others as a fish needs water."[22] Barth goes on to say that my humanity *also* depends upon the fact "that I need to *give*

---

21. See also chap. 6 of this volume.
22. Karl Barth, *Church Dogmatics* III/2 (Edinburgh: T. & T. Clark, 1960), 263.

my assistance to others as a fish needs water."[23] Thus Barth underscores Rosenberg's basic conviction that mutual and reciprocal care lies at the very heart of what it means to be human.

I believe that God's love is the wellspring from which we draw when we need compassion for ourselves or others. Not only Robert's caring presence toward me, but also my own ability to accept my human limitations, was finally sustained by a transcendent source of caring, the unfathomable abyss of God's love. Though my meditation began in deep grief, it led through the anguish for the tortured to compassion for myself and every human being who consents to bear a portion of the world's suffering. I was filled with gratitude for Robert and for all those willing to keep their hearts open in longing and vulnerability, to share in the suffering of our frail and fallen humanity.[24]

I believe that it is finally our connection to this transcendent source of compassion that enables us keep our hearts open in troubled times. When I am exhausted or confused or lost in a wilderness of sorrow, worry, or despair, I believe that there is One to whom I can turn for strength. In worship, in the great hymns and creeds of the church, in the comfort that comes from the simple compassion of another human being — in all these ways — I am comforted by the comfort of the gospel. For the New Testament presents Jesus Christ as One who has taken the suffering of the entire world into his own heart. He does not leave us to suffer the anguish of our mortal condition, nor the consequences of our sin, alone, but actively intercedes for us. Though I cannot fathom the depth of such a love, nor comprehend the mystery of his atoning sacrifice, nevertheless I am able to anchor myself in a transcendent ground for hope, a vision of the redemption of the entire world. Like the saints who have gone before us, I, too, long for the kingdom of God to come on earth as it is in heaven, where all human needs matter and every human need is fulfilled: a great banquet where the human family feasts in mutual joy.

---

23. Barth, *Church Dogmatics* III/2, 264.

24. While empathy and self-empathy are interlocking technical skills, compassion, in terms of one's willingness to suffer with others, "is only possible for us in and through our relationship with God." Purves, *The Search for Compassion*, 12.

81

Concluding Remarks

In this chapter I have sought to introduce a spiritual practice that has given me hope in a time when I desperately needed to be anchored in hope. The events following 9/11 have compelled me to dig more deeply in an attempt to be equal to the times. How do we keep our own spirits alive and not plunge into a sea of despair? My ability to speak out followed my willingness to enter a cauldron of grief and rage. Until I was able to have compassion for my own suffering, I was paralyzed by the frozen grief in my soul.

The prophetic witness and action to which we are called as Christians cannot endure without a willingness to suffer with those who suffer. Yet we cannot do this work with a glad heart unless we know how to drink regularly from the wellspring of God's compassion for all people. Those of us who work as pastors, counselors, or human helpers know that mourning is itself the work of healing. Active, fully engaged mourning, crying out in lament to God, is precisely what enables us to keep our hearts open in troubled times because we thereby open ourselves to the immeasurable compassion of God for each vulnerable human heart.

CHAPTER 5

Prayers of Lament

"How Long, O Lord?"

Prayers of lament arise *in extremis*. When the people of God undergo trial and cry out for deliverance, lament is faith's alternative to despair. It is a peculiar form of petitionary prayer, one that springs from unrelieved suffering. When healing fails, lament is the hopelessness that refuses to give up hope. When injustice prevails, lament is the protest that digs in for the long haul. When humiliation abounds, lament is the self-respect that cries out to a hidden God, "How long, O Lord?" Lament bends anguish and anger into ardent supplication. Sometimes it is no more than an inarticulate cry.

Lament is fueled by human longings, whatever they may be. Why does one woman lament over her inability to conceive a child while another can accept that a child is not given? Why does one member of a family still grieve for a beloved but lost brother, refusing to be consoled? Why does a man of faith persist year after year with the same plea to God, refusing to let go of a dream that seems within reach but is nevertheless withheld? Those who cry out to God in lament refuse to quench their desire. They are like the nuisance in Jesus' parable, who wrenches his neighbor from a warm bed in the dead of night to filch three loaves of bread for his visitors. They are like the importunate woman who so wears down the judge that he gives in just to be rid of her. Jesus admonishes his disciples never to give up hope but to persist in their entreaty to God, that their petitions may be heard. For if even an unjust human judge gives in to such importunity, how much more will the righteous Judge of the universe listen to their cries?

Yet, how long can lament persist? Over time, hope and despair seem to hang in the balance. The more fervent the hope, the more insistent the whisper of despair. Lament risks everything on God. It refuses the shell of cynicism that would protect its vulnerable heart. Instead, it remains open, alive, desiring, and therefore suffering. Think of Hannah in her longing for a son. Despite the ridicule of Eli, the priest, and the protestations of Elkanah, her husband, Hannah refuses to relinquish her desire. Though she has a husband who loves her tenderly, she weeps and refuses to be comforted. Recall the details as related in 1 Samuel. Elkanah has a second wife, Peninnah, who has been blessed abundantly with both daughters and sons. She flaunts her children, puffing herself up and shaming Hannah for her childlessness. Month after month, year after year, Hannah remains barren. When the family undertakes their annual pilgrimage to Shiloh to offer sacrifices, Peninnah taunts Hannah so that Hannah burns with desire for a son. The temptation to repress the desire must surely be present. But Hannah persists. Her husband protests, "Hannah, why do you weep? And why do you not eat? And why is your heart sad? Am I not more to you than ten sons?" No matter how sincere, Elkanah is powerless to change his wife's heart. She yearns for a son.

Hannah brings her lament to God when she offers her sacrifice in the temple. She weeps bitterly, prays in distress, and vows that if she is granted a son, she will offer him back to the Lord, to serve in the temple all his days. Eli sees her lips moving and reprimands her for drunkenness. But she protests; she is not drunk, only praying in distress. Eli answers, "Go in peace, and the God of Israel grant your petition which you have made to him" (1 Sam. 1:17). Trusting in the promise as spoken through the priest, Hannah is no longer sad. As promised, the Lord opens her womb and grants her a son, whom she names Samuel. As the Lord is faithful to her, so Hannah keeps her vow to the Lord. After weaning her firstborn, she returns to the temple in Shiloh and dedicates him to a lifetime of service.

We are familiar with Hannah's song about God's faithfulness in hearing the lowly. Hymns of joy supplant long nights of sorrow. The joy is proportional to the suffering that precedes it.

> Weeping may tarry for the night,
>> but joy comes with the morning.   (Ps. 30:5)

Yet how long does the night endure? A professor once described the eight years it took to write his dissertation as "an unhappy moment in my life." The endless prospect was in retrospect an "unhappy moment." How can such "moments" be borne?

Holy Scripture trains the church in hope. The Bible is very largely a story of hope emerging from hopelessness, of new beginnings arising from bitter endings. With the resurrection of Christ as the interpretive key, Scripture testifies that God comes to those who have lost all hope. Waters spring forth in the lifeless valley of Baca (Ps. 84). Rejected people are claimed for the work of God. Against all odds, slaves and prisoners are set free. Joseph is delivered from the pit, and the brothers who abandoned him are forgiven.

Lament means directing one's anguish toward God. Left to its own devices, the church is vulnerable to losing sight of hope. It is prone to forget the Creator who gives life itself, the Redeemer who forgives sin, and the Spirit who sustains it in hope. Jesus Christ releases his people from the burden of harm, both given and received, that would otherwise ensnare them in consequences beyond repair. God redeems the past by using what was meant for evil to bring good (Gen. 50:15-21). This is the tacit knowledge that sustains lament. Lament presupposes the majesty of God, his power to bring new life, and his compassion on all he has created. Lament is the last refuge of courage that hopes in God.

Psalms of Lament

In Psalm 88, arguably the most hopeless of the lament psalms, the psalmist writes,

> Thy wrath lies heavy upon me,
>> and thou dost overwhelm me with all thy waves.
> Thou hast caused my companions to shun me.   (vv. 7-8)

Yet if God has so afflicted him, why does he cry out day after day to this very God?

> O LORD, my God, I call for help by day;
>> I cry out in the night before thee.   (v. 1)

The psalmist not only laments the troubles of his life, the nearness of death, and his abandonment by friends and companions. He tells all this specifically to God, whose wrath afflicts him sorely. Then, in a series of ironic, almost mocking questions, he addresses God as Lord of the living:

> Dost thou work wonders for the dead?
>> Do the shades rise up to praise thee?

Is thy steadfast love declared in the grave?
   or thy faithfulness in Abaddon?
Are thy wonders known in the darkness,
   or thy saving help in the land of forgetfulness?   (vv. 10-12)

The questions are hardly a request for information. They push God to remember his identity. Is he not the One who works wonders, whose steadfast love is declared daily in prayer, liturgy, and song?[1] Surely God has not forgotten himself. The complaint reminds God that he is the Savior of Israel, the protector of his people. Though God has visited calamity upon them, his is the power of deliverance. The God of judgment is nevertheless the God of grace. There is nowhere else to turn.

Psalm 13 shows how a lament psalm is structured. In only six verses, it sets forth the major elements of lament:[2]

How long, O LORD? Wilt thou forget me for ever?
   How long wilt thou hide thy face from me?
How long must I bear pain in my soul,
   and have sorrow in my heart all the day?
How long shall my enemy be exalted over me?
Consider and answer me, O LORD my God;
   lighten my eyes, lest I sleep the sleep of death;
lest my enemy say, "I have prevailed over him";
   lest my foes rejoice because I am shaken.
But I have trusted in thy steadfast love;
   my heart shall rejoice in thy salvation.
I will sing to the LORD,
   because he has dealt bountifully with me.

The psalmist constructs his lament in three sections: the introduction, the body, and the conclusion. He begins by invoking God with urgency: How long will the Lord forget him? Will it be forever? One is not left to wonder about the complaint. All the lament psalms plunge the reader into the immediacy of abandonment.

---

1. See Patrick Miller, *They Cried to the Lord: The Form and Theology of Biblical Prayer* (Minneapolis: Fortress, 1994), 70.
2. See Miller, *They Cried*, 99-102.

86

My God, my God, why hast thou forsaken me?   (Ps. 22:1)

Why dost thou stand afar off, O LORD?
    Why dost thou hide thyself in times of trouble?
                                                              (Ps. 10:1)

At the same time, a level of intimacy is presupposed. The verbs in the imperative ("Consider and answer me, O LORD my God; / lighten my eyes")
are not ones that would be used with a stranger or mere acquaintance.
They imply an existing relationship. They address someone accessible. So
here with God. The imperatives presuppose a God who is known, loved,
and expected to help.

The body of the lament specifies the psalmist's distress, usually followed by a petition. In Psalm 13, pain and sorrow, triumphant enemies,
and the nearness of death are the complaints. The psalmist importunes
an answer from God: "Consider and answer me." Other laments urge God
to action, protest innocence, or remind God of past saving deeds. The
psalmist vows fidelity to the God who delivers him.

The conclusion indicates answered prayer, without showing how the
psalmist moves from suffering to release. Mysteriously, the prayer is heard.
The occasion for sorrow has become an occasion for joy. Here the psalmist
proclaims,

I will sing to the LORD,
    because he has dealt bountifully with me.

Something has shifted dramatically, for the psalmist has turned to song.
The trial is over. The psalmist turns from the past toward the future in
thanksgiving for the Lord's bountiful grace.

Psalm 13 is structured in a form known as chiasmus. In the ancient
world, thought was not always structured syllogistically in a linear fashion, as one would expect today: if A and B, then C follows, with C repre-
senting the culmination of the argument. Rather, A is paired with A' at the
beginning and end of the constructed unit. B is paired with B' moving in
toward the center, through C and C' to the cross-point. The Greek letter
chi (as in *chi*asmus) looks like the letter *X*, which is the center point of
the construction. If the psalm follows such a chiastic structure, one would
expect to see paired words or themes at the beginning and end of the

piece, with the most important point being made in the middle. Psalm 13 pairs three themes through the repetition of words before coming to the cross-point.

> A: How long, O LORD? Wilt thou forget me for ever?
> How long wilt thou hide thy face from me?
> B: How long must I bear pain in my soul,
> and have sorrow in *my heart* all the day?
> C: How long shall *my enemy* be exalted over me?
> X: Consider and answer me, O LORD my God;
> lighten my eyes, lest I sleep the sleep of death;
> C′: lest *my enemy* say, "I have prevailed over him";
> lest my foes rejoice because I am shaken.
> B′: But I have trusted in thy steadfast love;
> *my heart* shall rejoice in thy salvation.
> A′: I will sing to the LORD,
> because he has dealt bountifully with me.

The psalm begins and ends, in A and A′, with the psalmist's attention on the Lord. At the beginning, he cries out in supplication; at the end, his cries have turned to song. What begins as lament ends as praise. In B and B′, the psalmist's attention is on his own heart. In B he has sorrow in his heart, whereas in B′ his heart rejoices. In C and C′, as the psalmist moves toward the center, his focus is on his enemy. In C the enemy is exalted over him; whereas in C′ the factual shifts to a hypothetical; no longer a fact, the enemy now would only prevail if the Lord fails to answer. The center verse is in the imperative:

> Consider and answer me, O LORD my God;
> lighten my eyes, lest I sleep the sleep of death.

The center of the lament is the direct, desperate cry to God for help. The psalmist calls upon him as "my" God, making a claim of intimacy and describing the extremity of his peril.

The time sequences shift. The psalmist asks his anguished question in the present, looking back over a long stretch of the past. The present pain and sorrow are a reality of long suffering, sweeping over a vast arc of time: "all the day." The present perfect (as the past continuing into the present), "I *have* trusted," then shifts in hope toward the future: "My heart *shall* rejoice." Then, reversing the order, the future is juxtaposed once again with the present perfect:

> I *will sing* to the LORD,
> because he *has dealt* bountifully with me.

The shifting from present to past to future is a typical feature of the lament form. Psalm 126, for example, begins with the words

> When the LORD restored the fortunes of Zion,
> we were like those who dream.   (v. 1)

Thus it seems that Israel is looking back in time, remembering their deliverance. The psalmist recalls how their

> mouth was filled with laughter,
> and [their] tongue with shouts of joy.   (v. 2)

But then suddenly, the tenses shift. No longer are they looking back with joy, but they cry out to God in the present: "Restore our fortunes, O LORD," they call, "like the watercourses in the Negeb!" (v. 4). They seem to be in a situation of trial, calling upon God's name. The perpetual shuttling among present desperation, past deliverance, and anticipated rescue is a characteristic mark of biblical faith that is structured into the very pattern of the lament psalms.[3] God can be trusted, this mode of depiction suggests, because he fulfills his promises; God comes when he will, even when all human possibilities are spent. Again and again the psalms instruct the church to wait upon God, to call upon the Lord in its day of trouble. Lament sustains it in hope because the prayer is a living membrane that connects the people to God and God's steadfast love.

Psalms of lament are both corporate and personal. There are laments for the entire nation of Israel (e.g., Ps. 137: "How shall we sing the LORD's song / in a foreign land?") as well as for a single sufferer (e.g., Ps. 102, described as "the prayer of one afflicted, when he is faint and pours out his complaint before the Lord"). Liturgically, the most well-known lament may be Psalm 22, the prayer of Jesus from the cross: "My God, my God, why hast thou forsaken me?" In this prayer, Jesus gives voice to all hu-

---

3. Miller, *They Cried*, 68-86.

manity's lament over God's absence in time of need. Hughes Oliphant Old expresses it this way: "In his Passion Jesus himself prays the psalms of lamentation. When he offered himself up on the cross in that perfect act of worship, he presented to the Father the psalms of lamentation that Israel had prayed for a thousand years, and in those psalms were the cries of all humanity."[4] Here the personal and corporate are joined as Jesus conveys the human cry of anguish to the Father.

Worship is especially rich in prayers of lament during Holy Week, for that's when the innocent suffering of Christ joins collective human guilt. Through the cross of Jesus Christ, God takes the sin of the world into himself and suffers its consequences. Jesus drinks the bitter cup of god-forsakenness by undergoing the worst human suffering imaginable — an unjust execution for crimes not committed, betrayal and abandonment by friends, derision from enemies, physical torture, and public humiliation. When the church enters into the solemn mysteries of Holy Week, it confesses its participation in the human sin that cost the Son of God so dearly. Prayers of lament knit human sorrow over sin together with the suffering of loss and abandonment. The church beholds Jesus on the cross as both God and human being. He is the Son of God who suffers for the world in order to atone for its sin. At the same time, he is the Son of Man who suffers with the world the terrible plight of abandonment by God, persecution, and death. The cross of Jesus Christ is God's response not only to the guilt of human sin, but also to the terror and shame of human suffering.

At the heart of lament is a conflict felt by the person of faith who undergoes rending loss or extended trial. "If there is a just and loving God watching over his children, why doesn't he deliver them?" The prayer of lament does not avoid, but rather enters into, this tension between the experience of evil and faith's affirmation of the goodness of God. Lament takes this tension right to the breaking point, to a vision of God's eschatological rescue. Believing that the Lord is both loving and righteous, both mighty and gracious, the cry of lament cannot help but be a part of the landscape of faith because of the continuing presence of evil in the world. The loss of loved ones evokes anguish and incomprehension. Nicholas Wolterstorff, who lost his twenty-five-year-old son in a mountaineering accident, writes movingly about this anguish:

---

4. Hughes Oliphant Old, *Leading in Prayer: Workbook for Worship* (Grand Rapids: Eerdmans, 1995), 80.

I have no explanation. I can do nothing else than endure in the face of this deepest and most painful of mysteries. I believe in God the Father Almighty, maker of heaven and earth and resurrecter of Jesus Christ. I also believe that my son's life was cut off in its prime. I cannot fit these pieces together. I am at a loss. I have read the theodicies produced to justify the ways of God to man. I find them unconvincing. To the most agonized question I have ever asked I do not know the answer. I do not know why God would watch him fall. I do not know why God would watch me wounded. I cannot even guess.[5]

Rationalistic explanations fail to do justice to the heart's anguished cry of "Why?" Lament alone gives hope. By God's grace, the prayer of lament enables one to keep the question alive. By keeping the channel to God open, lament enables the unendurable to be endured. Kathleen Billman and Daniel Migliore, authors of *Rachel's Cry,* elaborate:

> The prayer of lament is a vivid reminder that persons can survive the disintegration of their previously unquestioned theological frameworks. What endures beyond the collapse of the frameworks is the relationship with the living God, a relationship strong enough for the telling of truth. . . . It is the deepening of that relationship with the living God that is the goal of pastoral care, and it is to that end that the prayer of lament has its place in Christian life and ministry.[6]

Lament in the Book of Job

Job is afflicted by every kind of evil: physical pain, the catastrophic loss of loved ones and worldly goods, social ostracism and public humiliation, enemies who taunt him, and friends who accuse him outright of secret sins. Though his anguish is multifaceted, Job remains notably single-minded. Throughout the narrative, Job insists on hearing from God alone. He calls upon God repeatedly in the most intense lament in Scripture. He rejects his friends as "miserable comforters" who only compound his suffering. He knows that he has to do with God and God alone. His friends act as if

---

5. Nicholas Wolterstorff, *Lament for a Son* (Grand Rapids: Eerdmans, 1987), 67-68.

6. Kathleen Billman and Daniel Migliore, *Rachel's Cry: Prayer of Lament and Rebirth of Hope* (Cleveland: United Church Press, 1999), 140.

they speak on God's behalf, which only exasperates Job. In the end God acknowledges that they did not "speak what is right" concerning him.[7]

The prologue makes clear that the calamities visited upon Job are not due to any sin of his, known or unknown. Therefore, when Job insists on his innocence —

> "There is no violence in my hands,
>   and my prayer is pure"   (16:17)

readers know that Job speaks truthfully but his friends do not. Indeed, they are scandalized. How can he so blatantly insist on his own innocence? How can he accuse God? They cannot see beyond their conviction that the morally upright are blessed and the wicked are punished. According to them, the universe operates according to this inviolable law.

Job excoriates them in turn for being full of "windy words." If their roles were reversed, he would not preach pious platitudes, nor presume to speak for God. On the contrary, he would give solace to the afflicted. He turns from them in disgust and directs his lament solely to God. He knows that consolation can come only from beyond. God alone can address him in his affliction. Surely no one but God can answer his questions of "Why?" and "How long?" When Job appeals to God as his witness against God his persecutor, the pattern of prayer from the Psalter reappears. Rather than fleeing *from* God as his enemy, he appeals *to* God as the one who will vindicate him. He appeals to God for help even though he believes God is persecuting him. He cries out,

> "O earth, cover not my blood,
>   and let my cry find no resting place.
> Even now, behold, my witness is in heaven,
>   and he that vouches for me is on high. . . .
>   My eye pours out tears to God,
> that he would maintain the right of a man with God,
>   like that of a man with his neighbor."   (Job 16:18-21)

The image of the witness in heaven comes from the ancient Israelite custom whereby a kinsman must avenge the blood of one killed unjustly. His

---

7. See Karl Barth, *Church Dogmatics* IV/3 (Edinburgh: T. & T. Clark, 1960), 383-88, 398-408, 421-34, 453-61.

blood, if left uncovered, will continue to cry out for revenge; his spirit will not rest until the death is avenged. Since there is no earthly kinsman to intercede for Job, who will take up his case and pursue justice? Who will demonstrate his innocence once and for all? Job boldly asks God to be his kinsman to defend his honor. Paradoxically, he calls on God to defend him against God.

As a man who fears God and understands his promises, Job knows that God is the defender of the defenseless, the protector of the innocent, and the lover of the poor. Therefore, God will be his witness, his defender, his redeemer. Despite all contrary evidence, Job casts himself on God as the only One who can vindicate him. Much the same occurs in Psalm 88 when the psalmist reminds God of his own character. Pointed questions are raised about God's ability to work wonders, his praiseworthiness among his people, his steadfast love, and his saving help toward all who call upon him. Like Job, the psalmist appeals to God against God, reminding him of his essential identity.

All the dramatic tension builds toward the direct encounter between Job and God. Job insists on fighting his wife, his friends, and even God himself until he receives the needed answer. The tenacity of his faith is fierce. Job relinquishes neither his claim to righteousness nor his insistence that the Almighty speak. The climax comes when, out of the whirlwind, God does in fact speak to Job. Sovereign and free, God vindicates Job before his friends. Yet his address is incomprehensible to the reader.

All we see in the foreground is a demonstration of God's power and might. We don't see the hidden work of the Holy Spirit. As in the psalms, so also here, a shift of attitude in the one praying lies hidden in the encounter with God. Real change occurs. Beyond all expectation, Job is satisfied with God's response. Having insisted so relentlessly on his innocence, Job astonishes the reader with humble repentance. What is it, one wonders, that prompts Job to repent in dust and ashes? What does he hear that causes him to rest his case?

The transition that the reader sees in Job — from angry lament to humble acknowledgment of God's majesty — is reminiscent of that in the psalms when cries of anguish turn into shouts of joy. Though Job hardly shouts with joy, the shift in attitude is nevertheless dramatic. The transition is perplexing. We do not know *what* occurs in the spiritual encounter. We only see *that* something occurs. The meaning of the encounter is shrouded in mystery. Yet this is so with each human soul and God. There is a holy inviolability in each person's encounter with God. Prayer can bring the sanctification of anguish even when one's plea is refused. Prayers for healing, when healing does not come, are then sustained by a "hope beyond healing."[8] Prayer points toward something mysterious that changes the human heart.

A poem that appears in Wendell Berry's *A Timbered Choir* hints at this mystery. In the poem a man is lying in bed in the dark, praying. Berry writes, "He is a man breathing the fear / of hopeless prayer, prayed / in hope." And then, mysteriously, something moves him. What "causes him to stir / like the dead in the grave" — "his own love or / Heaven's, he does not know."[9] In remembering love, everything changes. He finds himself surrounded by love, and his connection to God is restored.

Pastoral Care and the Prayer of Lament

The unique history that unfolds between God and Job is a paradigm for pastoral care. The decisive encounter is shown not to be between the caregiver and the afflicted, but between the afflicted one and God. When faced with Job-like suffering, caregivers are wise to avoid the judgmentalism of Job's "miserable comforters." They cannot be the judge of another's calamities, or interpret them as God's punishment. The God who alone sees the human heart is the God who alone may judge. Rather than standing in the place of God, caregivers need to stand alongside the afflicted, helping them to articulate their lament. "Whether or not the cries of pain and protest are identified as prayer by the afflicted, when suffering is experienced in the presence of God, the prayer of lament is in the process of formation. The caregiver's role is to hear and help bring this prayer to voice."[10]

When evil is overwhelming, Eugene Peterson says, pastoral care becomes "an assignment to share experiences of suffering."[11] The sufferer cannot simply put the tragedy behind him. There is no convenient "moral of the story" to be sought. No meaning can be found until each detail finds its place in a meaningful whole. To illustrate his point, Peterson examines Israel's suffering, as expressed in Jeremiah's Lamentations. These lamentations

---

8. Dale Aukerman, *Hope beyond Healing: A Cancer Journal* (Elgin, Ill.: Brethren Press, 2000).

9. Wendell Berry, *A Timbered Choir: The Sabbath Poems, 1979-1997* (Washington, D.C.: Counterpoint, 1998), 181.

10. Billman and Migliore, *Rachel's Cry*, 139.

11. Eugene Peterson, *Five Smooth Stones for Pastoral Work* (Atlanta: John Knox, 1980), 114.

are not marked by an amorphous primal scream. Instead, actual events are recounted — the siege of Jerusalem, the deadly famine, the flight of the king, the looting of the temple, and the dreaded exile. Names, places, and dates are a way of "tethering suffering," lest the framework of history dissolve. "History is necessary," Peterson observes, "not to explain, but to anchor."[12]

Caregivers who attend to those in distress are not there to explain the origin of the suffering, as Job's friends sought to do, or to minimize its impact. They are there simply to share it and to convey it to God. Peterson writes: "Pastors have no business interfering with another's sorrow, or manipulating it. Suffering is an event in which we are particularly vulnerable to grace, able to recognize dimensions in God and depths in the self. To treat it as a *'problem'* is to demean the person."[13] Peterson contrasts a "therapeutic" attitude with a "pastoral" attitude. The one looks at suffering as something to be fixed by an expert; the other sees suffering as something to be faced honestly, encountered fully, and shared in community. Hospital chaplains and hospice workers know that it is an honor to be asked to share in another's sorrow.

While enduring a two-year prison term near the end of his life, Oscar Wilde struck a different tone from the witty, light repartee for which he is known. His cry from "out of the depths" is powerful:

> If, after I am free a friend of mine gave a feast, and did not invite me to it, I should not mind a bit. I can be perfectly happy by myself. With freedom, flowers, books and the moon, who could not be perfectly happy? Besides, feasts are not for me any more. I have given too many to care about them. That side of life is over for me, very fortunately, I dare say. But if after I am free a friend of mine had a sorrow and refused to allow me to share it, I should feel it most bitterly. If he shut the doors of the house of mourning against me, I would come back again and again and beg to be admitted, so that I might share in what I was entitled to share in. If he thought me unworthy, unfit to weep with him, I should feel it as the most poignant humiliation, as the most terrible mode in which disgrace could be inflicted on me. But that could not be. I have a right to share in sorrow, and he who can look at the loveliness of the world and share its sorrow, and realise something of the wonder of both, is in immediate contact with divine things, and has got as near to God's secret as any one can get.[14]

12. Peterson, *Five Smooth Stones,* 126.
13. Peterson, *Five Smooth Stones,* 139.
14. Oscar Wilde, *De Profundis* (London: Putnam, 1905), 125-26.

Pastoral care counts for little if it is not a form of sharing in another's sorrow, and so of being in contact with divine things, a drawing near to the secret of God. Wilde's suffering gave him a new sense of what matters most in life — along with "freedom, flowers, books and the moon," the friendship that issues in shared suffering. The beauty of the world and its sorrow are meant to be shared.

When one shares one's suffering with others, one receives true consolation. By contrast, when one is isolated, one's suffering increases. To know that someone one loved was cherished by others, to weep with that person and share the sorrow, draws one into human connection. The caregiver's role is to facilitate communication among those who grieve. Peterson speaks of moving from private lament to public acknowledgment, "transform[ing] what is individual into something corporate." He continues: "Most cultures show a spontaneous comprehension of this. The suffering person is joined by friends who join their tears and prayers in a communal lament. They do not hush up the sound of weeping but augment it. They do not hide the sufferer away from view but bring him or her out into the public square."[15] In the villages of Africa, communal lament is still the norm rather than the exception. When there is a death, the villagers crowd into the lanes, no matter the time of day or night, crying out, beating their breasts, and tearing at their garments. The family is given the gift of seeing their loss embodied communally. The cries that ring through the streets confirm the preciousness of the one who has died.

In North America today, it is not unusual for a person to die far from the place where he was born. Local people gather for the funeral, while family members fly in from miles away. Friends who learn of the death often must grieve alone, for they too live in far-flung places. At best, they may share their memories with someone who did not know the deceased. By comparison with the African villages, these communities seem threadbare and fragile. They lack the continuity of generations and are held together only by committed efforts to stay in contact. Few stories belong to the community as a whole. One may not even know those people who share one's loss. One writer expresses the difficulty of connection this way:

> Given how often I have moved, my community is widely scattered. I
> have close friends all over the world; none of them know each other. We

15. Peterson, *Five Smooth Stones,* 143.

have only our own brief intensities of common experience to bind us, our telephone calls and letters. Friendship is tethered to loss, dependent on mental reconstruction instead of daily enactment. Sometimes I feel stranded at the center of a fragmented orb, my life divided into a series of experiences and places that can never be brought together — except in the solitude of memory. My family too is deposited all over the continent. Crucial junctures in our lives take place in hospital hallways or over bad coffee in airports.[16]

Yet human beings need the strength that comes through shared sorrow. Self-sufficiency melts away in the face of catastrophe and loss. Each person needs to be surrounded by the love that transcends death. "When the community joins in the lament, sanction is given for the expression of loss — the outpouring of emotion is legitimized in such a way as to provide for catharsis and then renewal."[17] The church may be one of the few places left where norms of community life are still valued. When the church joins in the prayer of lament, each member is upheld, and each person's sorrow matters to all.

Concluding Personal Reflections

In *A Timbered Choir,* Wendell Berry includes a poem dedicated to his granddaughters who visited the Holocaust Museum on the day that Yitzhak Rabin was buried. The poem begins, "Now you know the worst / we humans have to know / about ourselves, and I am sorry." But it moves gracefully and powerfully from darkness to light: "If you will have the courage for love, / you may walk in the light. It will be / the light of those who have suffered / for peace."[18]

When I encountered this poem in the fall of 2001, not long after the events of September 11, I remembered the inarticulate pain I had felt when I first had to tell our young daughter what had happened to Jesus. "Now you know the worst we humans have to know about ourselves and I am

16. Deborah Tall, "Dwelling: Making Peace with Space and Place," in *Rooted in the Land: Essays on Community and Place,* ed. W. Vitek and W. Jackson (New Haven: Yale University Press, 1996), 107.

17. Tall, "Dwelling," 142.

18. Berry, *A Timbered Choir,* 192.

sorry." She was not quite four.[19] Christmas had come and gone, along with the several impromptu plays where Daddy had been instructed to play the part of "Jophus," I had been Mary, and she had been the baby Jesus. Now with Holy Week approaching, I found myself mute. How could I tell her that Jesus, whom she loved in such innocence, was betrayed by one of his closest friends, deserted by the rest, handed over to be killed, and left to die on a cross? I couldn't bear the thought of seeing the hurt in her eyes, nor hear her uncomprehending "Why?" I wanted to protect her from this story of inhumanity. But there it was, right in the middle of our faith, the cross of Jesus, not to be evaded.

In the early days after September 11, I walked around in a daze, unable to concentrate. Images of fire and collapsing towers and human beings diving headlong to the earth went ceaselessly through my mind. At night planes flew overhead and fear gripped my heart. Over and over again I imagined myself as a passenger on one of the planes that had crashed into the towers. I lay awake, imagining my way into the terrified hearts of the passengers, of the office workers at the World Trade Center, of those who jumped, or were burned or crushed, of those who escaped and those who failed to escape. The scene etched itself in my mind with a wordless horror, not unlike that of November 22, 1963.

Some pastoral counselors have been trained in what is called critical incident stress debriefing, a method of working with communities that have undergone a common trauma. As I listened to their stories after the events of September 11, I discerned a certain note that was sounded repeatedly. Never before had these helpers felt so personally challenged. Never before in entering a traumatized community — where there had been a fire, a murder, or other tragic event — had they themselves been so impacted. Previously they had been able to provide a calm and stable center, around which the community could give voice to its pain. Now the helpers themselves were reeling with grief. How could they be anchors when they themselves were stricken?

When a catastrophe of this magnitude is encountered, where are words to give it form and voice? None of us is sustained by the chatter of newscasters or the stories of eyewitnesses, and rarely by the reassurances of government officials. At such times, we need something more enduring. In his poem "Loaves and Fishes," David Whyte says, "People are hungry, /

---

19. Cf. Deborah van Deusen Hunsinger, "Vocation: A Joyous Task," in *Compass Points: Navigating Vocation* (Princeton: Princeton Theological Seminary, 2002), 23-26.

and one good word is bread / for a thousand."[20] The bread that sustained me was four good words from the Apostles' Creed. Neither sermon, nor anthem, nor the great hymns could penetrate the numbness that set in. But when we rose to say what we all knew by heart, I recited the creed up to those four: "He descended into hell." Then I could not speak. Here was the bread to sustain thousands: our Lord descended into hell. He himself loved each one who had met doom that day. The divine compassion knew no limit in what he was willing to suffer for our sake. The psalmist knew this:

> If I make my bed in Sheol, thou art there!
> If I take the wings of the morning
>   and dwell in the uttermost parts of the sea,
> even there thy hand shall lead me,
>   and thy right hand shall hold me.   (Ps. 139:8-10)

Our pain and terror and despair are knit into Christ's lamentation to God.

When Nicholas Wolterstorff lost his son, he entered a long night of grief. Questions about God's goodness, the mystery of evil, and the incomprehensibility of suffering assailed him. He wrestled, like Jacob, with God. When day finally dawned, Wolterstorff was led to see that "to believe in Christ's rising from the grave is to accept it as a sign of our own rising from our graves." He writes:

> Slowly I begin to see that there is something more as well. To believe in Christ's rising and death's dying is also to live with the power and the challenge to rise up now from all our dark graves of suffering love. If sympathy for the world's wounds is not enlarged by our anguish, if love for those around us is not expanded, if gratitude for what is good does not flame up, if insight is not deepened, if commitment to what is important is not strengthened, if aching for a new day is not intensified, if hope is weakened and faith diminished, if from the experience of death comes nothing good, then death has won. Then death, be proud.
>
> So I shall struggle to live the reality of Christ's rising and death's dying. In my living, my son's dying will not be the last word. But as I rise up, I bear the wounds of his death. My rising does not remove them. They mark me. If you want to know who I am put your hand in.[21]

---

20. David Whyte, *House of Belonging* (Langley, Wash.: Mary Rivers Press, 1997), 88.
21. Wolterstorff, *Lament for a Son*, 92-93.

As the church dares to love the world with an open heart, it will suffer for the world's sake. Yet, it is by sharing in suffering love that it finds its vocation in pastoral care. "For as we share abundantly in Christ's sufferings, so through Christ we share abundantly in comfort too" (2 Cor. 1:5). The mystery of participation, *koinonia,* is the mystery at the heart of this work. In its own small way, it attests that greater suffering by which the world is overcome and made new. This is indeed a strange comfort, but it brings comfort where no other will do. There is no lament outside the bounds of this comfort, and no comfort that is not deepened by lament.

CHAPTER 6

Practicing *Koinonia*

Life Together

One of the most powerful signs of Christ's resurrection in the early church was the profound unity experienced among his disciples. "Now the company of those who believed were of one heart and soul" (Acts 4:32). The depth of Christian fellowship that developed is understood to be one of the Spirit's most precious gifts. When Saint Paul wants to bless the Corinthian church with the gifts of the Holy Trinity, he writes: "The grace *(charis)* of the Lord Jesus Christ and the love *(agape)* of God and the fellowship *(koinonia)* of the Holy Spirit be with you all" (2 Cor. 13:14). The fellowship of community is understood to be a blessing of divine origin beyond human powers to create. What is first of all God's gift only subsequently becomes a human task or spiritual practice. While we cannot create community *(koinonia)* by merely willing it, we can gladly nurture it once we are blessed with its presence.

Christian community is subsequent and derivative because its primary locus is the communion of love and freedom that characterizes the intimate mutual indwelling among the members of the Holy Trinity: Father, Son, and Holy Spirit. Though the Father and the Son retain their distinct identity and personal integrity, they are united by the Holy Spirit, who not only makes them an indivisible unity but also actively brings their love into the world. Each member of the Trinity dwells wholly within each other member, establishing a bond of inseparable unity among them. God's love flows into the world, because God does not choose to exist simply for himself, but to be in fellowship with his creatures. His love is therefore the eternal source and ground of human community. The Holy Spirit not only binds the Father to the Son, but also binds Jesus Christ to the church, the members of the church to each other, and the church to the world.

Jesus Christ thus joins the vertical and horizontal dimensions of our life together, uniting us through the Spirit with God and one another. Because we belong to Jesus Christ, we belong to each other as well. In Christ, our relationships with each other become a means through which God cares for us and through which we grow in faith, hope, and love. *Koinonia* describes the spiritual fellowship that is enjoyed by those who are knit together as one body. Variously translated as "fellowship" or "communion," "partnership" or "community," it is the same word Paul uses to speak of the bread and the cup being a *participation (koinonia)* in the body and blood of Christ. We live in Christ and Christ lives in us by the Spirit's mediation of Christ's living presence. This participation *in Christ* enables us to have a part in his ministry in the world as a community joined together in love.[1]

The biblical witness attests that human beings were created to live in fellowship with one another. "It is not good that the man should be alone" (Gen. 2:18). "The picture of the solitary Adam in Genesis 2 is one of self-alienation rather than self-fulfillment. . . . The divine image is not a religious quality of the individual person, but a spiritual reality expressed through the interchange of persons in relation."[2] Yet, often in the church we find it difficult to see any evidence of the *koinonia* of the saints. Instead, we see interpersonal conflicts that lead to entrenched power struggles, denominational factions that give rise to gnawing anxiety about whether the church can hold together, pastors who exhaust themselves trying to resolve disputes among staff, chronic disappointment that feeds latent cynicism, and leaders who burn out and leave the church or act out and do widespread harm.

We confess in our creed, "I believe in the communion of saints," but we long for glimpses of it in our everyday life. How is our witness to be credible if we are constantly at odds with one another? How are we to grow in faith, hope, and love if we fail to acknowledge our need of one another? How can the *koinonia* we confess by faith become a living reality among us?

Because of our fallen condition, we will not likely see the complete living out of *koinonia* until the fullness of time. In the meantime, however, there are concrete practices that build up the church, that contribute to

1. Deborah van Deusen Hunsinger, *Pray without Ceasing: Revitalizing Pastoral Care* (Grand Rapids: Eerdmans, 2006), chap. 1: "A Theology of *Koinonia*."

2. Ray S. Anderson, *Self-Care: A Theology of Personal Empowerment and Spiritual Healing* (Wheaton, Ill.: Victor Books, 1995), 238.

koinonia's flourishing. At the very heart of our mysterious union in Christ lies our common life of worship, prayer, and participation in the sacraments. Weekly preaching of the gospel forms, informs, and transforms believers as it proclaims the living reality of Jesus Christ in the world. Prophetic action seeks to witness faithfully to signs of God's kingdom in our midst. In pastoral care, *koinonia* becomes visible when believers entrust one another with their burdens and afflictions, as well as their common vocation and hope.

Yet *koinonia* is often lacking in our routine, everyday interactions. How might the church truly become what it is called to be: a community of mutual care, healing, and hope? Are there skills and practices that can help us communicate in ways that contribute to the building up of trust, honesty, and mutual understanding?

Nonviolent Communication

For the past twenty-five years, I have taught a process of communication developed by Marshall Rosenberg called "nonviolent communication" (NVC), which teaches people how to listen with empathy and speak with honesty. When placed in a Christian theological framework, it is the best model I know for practical training in "speaking the truth in love." In this chapter I will seek to show how NVC nurtures a kind of consciousness and teaches a set of skills that can help people to live in glad fellowship with one another, respect one another in their differences, resolve their conflicts peacefully, and contribute to one another's well-being.

In the turbulent 1960s, Marshall Rosenberg, a clinical psychologist, decided to train ordinary people in skills of empathic communication. Disturbed by the violence he experienced as a child in Detroit, he sought to develop a model of communication that would contribute to cooperation and peace. For more than forty years, he has been involved in a range of educational and peacemaking activities, including acting as a mediator between Palestinians and Jews in the Middle East, between the Hutus and Tutsis in Rwanda, and between police and gang members in the inner cities of America. Though he clearly has a special *charism* for this work, I believe that he has developed an ingenious model for teaching the skills he embodies.

NVC has grown into an international training and peacemaking organization with teachers and trainers in eastern and western Europe, the

Middle East, Russia, Asia, Africa, and North and South America. It is taught in schools and prisons, in churches and community centers, in colleges and universities. Teachers have developed curricular materials to use with students ranging from kindergartners through high schoolers. Practice groups are springing up all over the world. I teach a course entitled "Developing Compassionate Communication in the Church" at Princeton Seminary in which NVC is central to learning the complex interpersonal, pastoral care, and leadership skills needed for ministry.

The overall aim of NVC is compassionate connection. The three major components for achieving a quality of mutual connection between parties are empathic reception, self-empathy, and honest expression. Each component has four steps: observation (O), feeling (F), need (N), and request (R). While these steps can be cognitively grasped relatively easily, the more challenging task of integrating them into one's ordinary functioning requires commitment. The third step, identifying needs, is the conceptual linchpin of the whole. Learning how to connect with one's own and others' needs is the key to transforming animosity or indifference into constructive, and sometimes even joyful, connections.

The first step is *observation*. Whenever we seek to communicate clearly with others, it is helpful first to let them know which of their words or actions in particular are affecting us. If we can describe what we are observing without at the same time evaluating it, connection is facilitated. Especially if we have a negative reaction to another's words or behavior, it helps simply to describe it with as little evaluative sense as possible. Negative judgments tend to evoke defensiveness. Observations describe what is available to our senses: what we can see, hear, touch, taste, and smell. They are specific to time and context.

If your friend arrives thirty minutes late for a two o'clock appointment, you might say, for example, "I'm puzzled because I have you down in my calendar for two o'clock." If you were to say instead, "You are always late for our appointments," you would obviously be mixing in an evaluation. Even apart from the inflammatory use of the word "always," you don't actually *know* that he is late; all you know is that your calendar says that he was due to arrive at two. He may have a different understanding about the time you were to meet. Separating your observation from any possible evaluation facilitates connection because it gives no offense. The intention in making an observation is to share helpful information about what in particular you are reacting to, not to criticize or lay blame at the other's door.

The second step in the NVC model is stating what you are *feeling*. We continually assess what is happening in our environment through our feeling capacities. Daniel Goleman, in his book *Emotional Intelligence,* argues that we are capable of appraising situations with lightning speed. Laboratories can now measure the interval between a stimulus and our emotional response to it in the thousandths of a second.[3] Such speed, says Goleman, helped guarantee human survival when even a millisecond might make the difference between life and death. If a snarling dog lunges toward me, my fear reaction will send hormones to my brain that will activate my fight, flight, or freeze response before I have time consciously to assess the dog's relative danger.

Besides acting as a kind of radar for danger, our emotions are also closely tied to our thoughts. Anyone who practices cognitive-behavioral therapy or mindfulness meditation will know how intimately interwoven our emotional state is with our beliefs, judgments, and thoughts. Many of our emotions are not triggered directly by a change in the environment, but rather by our rational assessment of that change. If I conclude that my accountant is cheating me, I would likely feel angry. However, if I realize that I have misinterpreted his report, my feelings would likely change. No longer believing that he is cheating me, I would feel relieved. The emotions I have depend on the cognitive assessment I make. Learning to take note of our intervening thoughts and to connect them with our emotions is a key skill in NVC.

NVC not only acknowledges the integral connection between feelings and thoughts, it also seeks deeper understanding by connecting feelings with *needs.* Assessing what we need is the third step of the NVC model. The key to developing a high level of NVC consciousness and skill lies in this step. It is a basic presupposition of NVC that we are trying to get our needs met in every moment. We are motivated to act, speak, keep silent, move toward or away from someone on the basis of our needs. Virtually everything we do (or fail to do) is an attempt to meet a need. Thus, our "needs" are the source of our underlying motivation. What are we desiring, wanting, working toward, hoping for, or valuing at any particular moment in time? If our basic needs are being met, we might feel (for example) contented, excited, relaxed, delighted, joyful, moved, or happy. If our basic needs are not being met, we might feel frustrated, angry, sad, discontented, bored, disappointed, or anxious. In the examples I have given, the pertinent need in relation to my accountant would likely be trust. The

---

3. Daniel Goleman, *Emotional Intelligence* (New York: Bantam Books, 2006), 23.

need regarding the snarling dog would be safety. The need regarding the appointment with your friend might be clarity or consideration, depending on how you assess the situation.

Needs by definition contribute to life. Though they are met in different ways in different cultures, needs themselves are universally shared. Thus all people have a need for food, water, clothing, warmth, and shelter. All human beings need rest. All persons have basic needs for safety, connection, community, support, respect, and understanding. People everywhere need hope and meaning. While Abraham Maslow identified a hierarchy of needs, suggesting that one cannot consider meeting the "higher" spiritual and emotional needs if one is hungry or thirsty, Viktor Frankl's remarkable book, *Man's Search for Meaning*, is persuasive in arguing that our need for meaning may be even more basic than our need for bread.[4]

Notice that this use of the term "need" is quite different from its common use, where being "needy" can be seen as shameful or weak. In a North American cultural ethos, many persons strive to be as "independent" as possible or to appear to be as free of needs as they can. In our culture one risks being labeled self-absorbed or selfish for trying to get one's needs met. One "shouldn't" ask for "too much." One student of NVC writes, "I *hate* needing other people and taking their time and energy. I hate it when I burden others with my pain."

By contrast, NVC teaches that needs are qualities that contribute to life, and that *it is a gift* to let others know what our needs are. To be connected to our needs is to be connected to our deep motivations, to the qualities of being that make life worth living. They do not point to a deficit, but rather to an abundance. Some NVC trainers speak of the "beauty of the needs" as precious qualities of human being.[5] To connect with a need is to connect with something desirable and life-giving. When "need" is understood as a fullness rather than a deficit, to connect with the need is to connect with a vital value or quality of soul.

For example, to connect with your need for affection, you might first become aware of its absence. Perhaps in recent weeks there has been little affection expressed between you and your spouse, and you find yourself

---

4. Viktor Frankl, *Man's Search for Meaning* (New York: Beacon Press, 2006). In Frankl's harrowing experience in a Nazi death camp, he kept hope alive through meaningful connections with others, which he believes was more fundamental to his survival than even his daily bread.

5. I first learned of the "beauty of the needs" from Dr. Robert Gonzales, whose teaching has greatly enriched my understanding of NVC as a spiritual practice.

longing for its return. Here to notice a "need" for affection is to experience it as a deficit. To connect with it as a life-giving value, by contrast, you might ponder how much you enjoy affection in your intimate relationships. You might remember specific moments of affection exchanged with those you love and become aware of the tenderness, gentleness, and warmth that characterized those interchanges. You might even connect with "the beauty of the need" by thinking about your dog welcoming you home with exuberant wet kisses. By connecting with the beauty of the need, you no longer focus on a particular person or situation but rather connect with the quality inherent in the need itself as something you value. The process entails finding access to its life-giving energy, in other words, whether or not it is currently a part of any particular relationship. When we connect with "the beauty of the need" in this way, we experience our longing for affection as something rich, multivalent, and full of meaning. It is something of great value, not something to be embarrassed by or ashamed of.

Sometimes the needs motivating our behavior lie completely outside of our awareness. This is especially true when we are "triggered" by another's words or actions that stimulate strong emotional reactions. Our feelings, according to Rosenberg, are never directly *caused* by another's action, but rather by our *own* underlying need. In the example of the "late" appointment, it is now 2:29 P.M. and your friend has not yet arrived. What might you be feeling? Annoyed? Worried? Relieved? You could be feeling any of these depending upon your need. If you want to know that your friend is safe or if you want clarity about the agreed-on time, you might be worried. On the other hand, if you want to use your time efficiently and begin thinking that your friend doesn't respect your time, you might feel annoyed, perhaps extremely so. But if you are needing rest, you might actually feel relieved that your friend has not yet arrived. You can take a much-needed break in the middle of the day and feel refreshed when he arrives. The source of your feeling thus lies in your need, whether for respect or clarity or rest, not in the other's actions. It is not the *fact* of your friend being later than you expected that is causing your feelings, in other words; it is how you *interpret* that fact in the light of your needs.

NVC assumes that what the other person does or says is never the *cause* of our feelings. What this means practically is that no one else ever "makes us" feel anything. We alone are responsible for our feelings. One writer has remarked that the other's actions are merely the detonator for our feelings, whereas our unmet need is the dynamite.[6] This quip points to those familiar situations where a seemingly small provocation can set off an apparently disproportionate reaction. If you have chronic unmet needs around a particular issue, your pain may get expressed quite vehemently in response to the slightest triggering event. Working with these kinds of triggering events therefore has rich potential to bring about healing and growth. It is well worth the effort to uncover and work constructively with chronically unmet needs. Having the skill to transform pain into an appreciation of one's core values or needs reframes the experience of being "triggered" altogether. Instead of withdrawing, analyzing, or lecturing oneself on one's obvious neurotic tendencies ("Here's that same stupid dynamic I've been trying to overcome for years"), one becomes curious, even intrigued, to investigate these signs of life sprouting up. One moves gently *toward* the pain, inquiring into it with a caring and open attitude. For underneath the grief, rage, or pain lies an unmet need that is of great importance.

The process of finding a strategy to address the need is the fourth step of the model. Once we have clarity about what we need, we can make a *request* that we believe will contribute to its being met. The request needs to be time-specific and doable, what Rosenberg calls positive action language. It is important to ask specifically for what you want, not for what you don't want. Thus, you might say, "I'd like you to call me once a week," *not* "I don't want you to call me so often." The request also needs to be specific and doable: "Would you be willing to give me a hug right now?" *not* "I'd like you to be more affectionate."

Rosenberg sometimes comments that you should never agree to fulfill another's request unless you can do so "with the gladness of a young child feeding a hungry duck." In other words, requests are understood as gifts, not as demands. They give us an opportunity to contribute to another's life, which Rosenberg believes is a fundamental human need. If you say no to someone's request, it is likely because you are saying yes to some unstated need of your own. Conversations around requests are thus opportunities to connect with one another about both persons' needs, which are equally valued in NVC. If the other responds to your no by blaming, coercing, ridiculing, or pleading with you, the request was secretly a demand. NVC jealously guards the freedom of each person's choice and seeks to avoid

6. Kelly Bryson, quoted in Jane Connor and Dian Killian, *Connecting across Differences* (New York: Hungry Duck Press, 2005), 83.

making demands. Any time you agree to do something out of fear, shame, or coercion and not freely or gladly, you build up resentment toward the other. You may "submit" now, only to "rebel" later. There is little chance for joyful fellowship with someone who uses his power over you to "make" you do something you do not wish to do.

Rosenberg coaches people how to hold on to their needs passionately but to be flexible and creative in finding strategies to meet them. If your spouse is too tired to go out dancing, the chances are that he needs rest. If you are needing fun and companionship, going dancing with your spouse is only one possible strategy. If you truly value both of your needs, other strategies can be considered. (You could go dancing with a friend, and your partner could stay at home and rest. You could play Scrabble with your partner tonight and go dancing over the weekend. You could gladly stay home and read him some poetry that makes both of you laugh.) Once your partner trusts that you want to honor his needs as much as your own, he may be glad to join you in brainstorming creative strategies (unless he is so desperately in need of rest that he is already asleep).

Honesty and empathy are the cornerstones of connection: honesty about what is going on in ourselves and empathy for others. If we are unable to connect with others' underlying needs, we cannot hear them with empathy. If we stand in judgment of them, or diagnose or label them in some way, we will fail to make an empathic connection. Obstacles to connection include language that denies choice: "you have to," or "you must not," or "you *should*"; language that expresses demands: "If you don't do this, I'll do that"; or language that threatens guilt: "If you don't do such and such, I'll feel so disappointed in you." Labeling also blocks compassionate connection: "Roger always tries to dominate our conversations; he has such a need for control."[7] Even clinical diagnoses can undermine empathic connection: "He acts that way because he is bipolar, or a sexual offender, or an alcoholic." Even if considered clinically accurate, the diagnosis prevents you from truly connecting with that person in the present moment.

Working through these four steps can seem mechanical or awkward, especially at first. Yet, even at their most mechanistic, they have the po-

7. To say that Roger has a "need for control" is labeling or "diagnosing" him rather than truly trying to discover his need. A so-called need for control is not a true need. What is generally interpreted as a need for control is usually a need for trust or empowerment or even contribution.

tential to change habitual dynamics for the better. Using the OFNR outline for developing skill is similar to practicing scales at the piano. If you want to make music, you need the daily practice. Using the steps as a mental guide facilitates clarity and contributes to ease in learning. Even a little OFNR can go a long way. Just as a simple Italian phrase book can find you a place to sleep, enable you to buy groceries, or allow you to navigate your way through an unknown city, so knowing the basics of OFNR can contribute to your life in fundamental ways. This is so because NVC helps you become aware of your habitual ways of communicating and provides ready tools for change. By consciously working through each of the steps, you may become aware, for example, how frequently you label or judge others, or how in certain situations you express your feelings without any real awareness of your underlying need. Or you may realize that certain feeling words are not in your vocabulary because they are somehow linked with feelings of shame. Long-standing patterns become readily apparent.

Compassionate Communication as a Christian Spiritual Practice

Marshall Rosenberg does not consider NVC to be a Christian practice, though he does emphasize its "spiritual" nature.[8] Rosenberg, a Jew by heritage, speaks of God as "Beloved Divine Energy," which is the basis for every human being's connection to life. For Rosenberg, NVC arises out of his desire to manifest love by connecting with the "Divine Energy" in himself and others. He writes:

> [I]f we get in touch with each other's Divine Energy, it's inevitable that we will enjoy giving and we'll give back to life. I've been through such ugly stuff with people that I don't get worried about it anymore, it's inevitable. If we get that quality of connection, we'll like where it gets us.
>
> It amazes me how effective it is. I could tell you similar examples between the extremist Israelis, both politically and religiously, and the same on the Palestinian side, and between the Hutus and the Tutsis. . . . With all of them it amazes me how easy it is to bring about this recon-

---

8. See https://www.cnvc.org/learn-online/spiritual-basis/spiritual-basis-nonviolent-communication, accessed March 13, 2014.

ciliation and healing. Once again, all we have to do is get both sides connected to the other person's needs. To me the needs are the quickest, closest way to getting in connection with that Divine Energy. Everyone has the same needs. The needs come because we're alive.[9]

Though Rosenberg does not officially align himself with any particular religion, he sees connection with the "divine" in himself and others as the goal of human existence. NVC trainers and practitioners around the world belong to every conceivable religion. In my local practice group, I listen empathically to a Hindu, a Buddhist, a Lutheran, a humanist, a Quaker, a Jew, a Greek Orthodox, and an agnostic. When we meet we focus not on these differences, but rather on our common humanity, by connecting with one another's feelings and needs.

Nevertheless, if I am going to commit myself to a spiritual practice, I want it to be congruent with my particular religious beliefs. Though I greatly value the way that NVC has enabled me to know and love people with a wide range of religious beliefs, I myself am interested in NVC because I want to be a faithful disciple of Jesus Christ. After years of study and practice, I have come to believe that NVC's fundamental principles are congruent with my understanding of the gospel.[10] The joyful mutual giving and receiving that Rosenberg describes as the goal of NVC can be understood as an image of redeemed humanity: not only how we were originally created to be but also how we will one day live in love, harmony, and fellowship *(koinonia)* with one another in the kingdom of God.

One of the key features of Karl Barth's theological anthropology is speaking and listening to one another with gladness. Others cannot know us unless we consent to making ourselves known. Others may be able to surmise something about us, but if we want to be fully human, we need to reveal ourselves. "This two-sided openness is the first element of humanity. Where it lacks, and to the extent that it lacks, humanity does not occur. To the extent that we withhold and conceal ourselves, and therefore do not move to know others and to let ourselves be known by them, our existence is inhuman."[11] Insofar as we seek to know and be known by the other, we

---

9. https://www.cnvc.org/learn-online/spiritual-basis/spiritual-basis-nonviolent-com munication, accessed March 13, 2014.

10. See Theresa F. Latini, "Nonviolent Communication and the Image of God," *Perspectives: A Journal of Reformed Thought* 22, no. 5 (May 2007): 10-16.

11. Karl Barth, *Church Dogmatics* III/2 (Edinburgh: T. & T. Clark, 1960), 251.

try to find a bridge, a way of connecting to the other. "I should not take him seriously as a human being if I did not seriously try to find the way from me to him."[12] Moreover, we engage in the mutual give-and-take of listening and speaking, as well as offering one another mutual assistance, "with gladness."

> What we indicate in this way is really the *secret* of humanity. . . . [I]n doing so we presuppose as the living center of the whole the decisive point that they meet gladly and in freedom. . . . [T]here is a discovery, the mutual recognition that each is essential to the other. . . . [There is] an active willing of this fellowship, a willing which derives quite simply from the fact that each has received a gift which he necessarily desires to reciprocate to the best of his ability. And if it is asked in what this gift consists, the answer must be that the one has quite simply been given the other, and that what he for his part has to give is again himself.[13]

Barth's "gladly" and "in freedom" can be seen to correspond to Rosenberg's desire to meet requests only when he can do so in pure gladness of heart. Both Christian theology and NVC recognize the importance of honoring the freedom of each person's choices and of understanding the "gift" character of our life together.

From a Christian perspective, the theological ground of compassionate listening is found in God's own listening to human hearts whenever we reach out to God in prayer. Scripture gives us countless instances of God's love being demonstrated through a listening responsiveness to human need. Bonhoeffer describes the integral connection between divine and human listening in his book *Life Together*. "The first service that one owes to others in the community involves listening to them. Just as our love for God begins with listening to God's Word, the beginning of love for other Christians is learning to listen to them. God's love for us is shown by the fact that God not only gives us God's Word but also lends us God's ear. We do God's work for our brothers and sisters when we learn to listen to them."[14] As we listen to others, we thereby witness to the love of the listening God and impart hope to those whose story has not yet been

---

12. Barth, *Church Dogmatics* III/2, 257.
13. Barth, *Church Dogmatics* III/2, 271-72.
14. Dietrich Bonhoeffer, *Life Together* (Minneapolis: Augsburg Fortress, 1996), 98.

fully articulated nor fully heard. Such deep listening brings both spiritual sustenance and emotional healing in its wake.

Dealing with Criticism

One of the places that *koinonia* breaks down, sometimes irretrievably, is when we are criticized by others. Take the example of a pastor who hears criticism from one of her parishioners. She might feel hurt and withdraw from the person who has criticized her, or she might lash back at him in anger. Alternatively, she might suppress her reaction and pretend not to be hurt or angry, only to express her ire to a third party, who is then "triangled in," which only serves to perpetuate the problem.[15] Yet, in the everyday reality of church life, what do church leaders do or say when their preaching, teaching, administrative style, or pastoral care is criticized? What are they to do with the frustration or anger that bubbles up or boils over as they hear others criticizing their sincere efforts? How might a skilled pastor adept at NVC deal with such criticism?

NVC teaches that it is possible to hear a message in four ways. First, one may hear the "critical" comment as simply something true about oneself. In this situation, the pastor might hear the negative judgment and immediately take it to heart, thinking: "I did a bad thing," or "I shouldn't have said that," or even "I can't believe what an idiot I am." Hearing a critical message in this way has the potential to perpetuate self-doubt, shame, or depression.

A second way to hear a critical comment is to defend oneself against it by blaming, discounting, diagnosing, or judging the messenger. "Who does he think he is, criticizing my sermon? He clearly doesn't have the intellectual interests that I have and so cannot possibly appreciate what I am trying to do in this situation." The pastor might think these things to herself, or she might say something directly to deflect the criticism: "Perhaps you are unaware of the controversy in the church that I am addressing here. There have been several articles in recent theological

---

15. Edwin Friedman, *Generation to Generation: Family Process in Church and Synagogue* (New York: Guilford Press, 1985), 37. Friedman shows how emotional triangles perpetuate stress in an emotional system and keep issues from being resolved. "The relationship of any two members of an emotional triangle is kept in balance by the way a third party relates to each of them or to their relationship. When a given relationship is stuck, therefore, there is probably a third person or issue that is part of the homeostasis."

journals that consider this an issue of great importance." Even if this is the reason the pastor chose a given topic for her sermon, she needs first to hear and understand what matters to her parishioner. By defending her choice instead of listening with empathy, she fails to learn what is at stake *for him*.

A third way of hearing criticism is for the pastor to offer *herself* empathy as she listens. She might say to herself, "Gosh, I feel so discouraged when I hear that. I worked hard on that sermon and really wanted to contribute to my congregation's understanding of what I consider to be one of the most important theological issues of our time." Notice how she is acknowledging her feeling (discouragement) and need (contribution) in this empathic statement to herself. By anchoring herself in the beauty of her own need, she is more likely to stay centered and calm as she listens to her parishioner.

A fourth way of hearing a critical message is to "translate" the parishioner's criticism into an empathic guess about *his* feelings and needs. The pastor can do this either silently or out loud. Thus, she might say, "Are you frustrated because you'd like to understand the relevance of my sermon for our church?" Or, "Are you feeling annoyed because you'd like some guidance in the kinds of dilemmas you confront in your daily life?" Here the pastor *doesn't even hear criticism* because her focus is exclusively on understanding the parishioner's feelings and needs. Even if he expresses intense frustration, she knows this is a sign that what is at stake (his underlying need) matters a great deal to him. The pastor hears, not that there is something wrong with her (or her sermon), but rather how fervently her critic longs for a faith that is relevant. Heard in this way, his message would not be a source of discouragement but rather an opportunity to connect meaningfully with what really matters in the life of faith. With NVC skills in hand, the pastor would be so adept at hearing criticism that she would not even hear it as criticism. Instead, she would hear the honest expression of another person's heartfelt values and longings.

If, by contrast, she were to react with anger and criticism (or self-blame and self-criticism), she could still return to the subject later, listening once again for feelings and needs. If she were to lash out with a countercriticism or defend her choice, that means she is likely caught in judgment and blame, which are generating her feelings of anger. Here Jesus' words offer wisdom and guidance. "Judge not, and you will not be judged; condemn not, and you will not be condemned; forgive, and you will be forgiven; give, and it will be given to you; good measure, pressed down, shaken together, running over, will be put into your lap. For the measure you give will be the measure you get back" (Luke 6:37-38). Insofar as she is judging herself or the other, she has not fully connected either with her underlying need or his. To work with her own anger constructively, she would first need to be brutally honest about *her own* judgments. What are the thought processes that are feeding her anger? For instance, she might be thinking: "He shouldn't be so critical. He has no idea how hard that sermon was for me to write. He has also completely misunderstood my message." This set of thoughts can be "translated" into feelings and needs as follows: "I am so discouraged because I'd like some appreciation for my efforts. It took quite a bit of courage to preach that sermon. I wanted to help my congregation see how certain global issues are integrally connected to our life of faith." Once she fully understands *her own needs* for appreciation and contribution, she can develop other strategies to address those needs. In other words, she would not set all her hopes on getting that particular parishioner to appreciate her contribution. Instead, she might ask a colleague for feedback on what he considers the sermon's strengths to be. In addition, she might explore the pain involved in not being heard with her own intention (his "misconstruing the message"), exploring the possibility that his comment is "charged" for her because it stimulates one of her own chronically unmet needs. Her deeper need may be for reconciliation with someone in her past who repeatedly triggered pain over her unmet needs for understanding.

Surprisingly, just recognizing her own unmet needs in the situation has the potential immediately to defuse her anger. Once she fully acknowledges her need for appreciation, she can actually go on *to appreciate herself* for writing the sermon she wrote. In acknowledging her courage in giving this particular sermon, she has already begun to meet her own need for appreciation. Doing this process of self-empathy is very different from justifying herself or refusing to see her parishioner's point of view. In connecting with her own needs, she grounds herself so fully that she is then able to see that even though *she* appreciates what she set out to do, this particular parishioner's needs were not met in this instance. If she appreciates her own intention fully and gives herself the understanding she desires, she doesn't have to become defensive because her parishioner didn't get what he had hoped for on this particular occasion. Once connected with her own life energy, she is free to explore his more fully. She can look for the vibrant beauty of his needs with openheartedness. What might have begun as an alienated, distant, or conflicted relationship can thereby blossom into one characterized by mutual understanding and appreciation. The more clearly she listens to his feelings and needs, the more deeply connected she will be to what matters to him about his faith and his participation in the church. *Koinonia* will be restored.

Avoiding Pastoral Burnout and Misconduct

Of critical concern for those in ministry (as well as for the institutions that educate and sustain them) are the issues of pastoral burnout and sexual acting out. Some pastors regularly work sixty or more hours a week, fail to take a Sabbath day of rest, do not replenish themselves with worship (where they can simply be participants), have few friends, and are cut off from an inner sense of what they need. In addition, in the line of duty, they may experience the vicarious trauma of those suffering from tragic loss or victimized by violence. "Ministry is dangerous," writes Margaret Kornfeld, "for those who are disconnected from themselves."[16] Ministers may be starving emotionally or spiritually and not know it. Because their duties encourage them to become absorbed in the lives of others, they can easily lose track of their own lives. Indeed, they may be completely oblivious to their own needs until those needs clamor for attention through burnout or acting out. Kornfeld captures some of the dynamics involved. "Those who burn out often have an insatiable internal system that requires them to give to others in order to fill an inner void. At the beginning of their calling, the void seems to be filled by the community's appreciation of their outreach and caregiving. But eventually, they feel empty again and so they try harder to give to others, repeating what has not worked, leaving them exhausted."[17] Such pastors experience chronic stress in their work without ever really identifying it. This kind of stress can be ameliorated by the simple practice of connecting with their own needs and then searching for reliable strategies to meet them.

Pastors need friends with whom they can be themselves apart from their pastoral role. Putting friends as their lowest priority, far below effectiveness and productivity in their work, is a telltale sign of the breakdown of *koinonia*. As they get caught up in busyness, many also stop drinking deeply from the well of Scripture and prayer, except to prepare their next sermon or class. Bonhoeffer's advice to seminarians addresses this temp-

---

16. Margaret Kornfeld, *Cultivating Wholeness: A Guide to Care and Counseling in Faith Communities* (New York: Continuum, 1998), 281.

17. Kornfeld, *Cultivating Wholeness*, 283.

tation. In his book *Meditating on the Word,* Bonhoeffer writes, "Do not ask how you should tell it to others, but ask what it tells you!"[18]

Sexual misconduct by a pastor or church leader shakes entire congregations to the core, bringing widespread disillusionment, acute pain, and mistrust in its wake. At the heart of sexual acting out lies a similar ignorance about one's own needs. Ministers who stay in their pastoral role around the clock, having few intimate companions with whom they can simply be themselves, are in danger of losing connection with who they are. If they are starving for emotional contact and yet are unaware of their own needs, they will be drawn to the vulnerability of those who come to them for help. There they can play a "heroic" role of helping the other while remaining essentially unaware of how much they themselves long for emotional closeness. Sexual misconduct is often preceded by inappropriate self-disclosure on the part of the pastor,[19] a sure sign that the pastor is emotionally isolated, with too few friends to confide in. Other "signs" and "signals" of personal distress go unheeded when the pastor fails to acknowledge his (or her) feelings and needs. Feelings of resentment or bitterness, conflict that is chronic and unresolved, persistent feelings of paralysis or helplessness, cynicism or depression, reliance on status or prestige as a core source of self-esteem, recurring sexual fantasies or fantasies of emotional intimacy with a particular person, painful difficulties in one's own marriage or family of origin that are not fully faced — all these are warning signs for potential burnout or acting out. In each case, the pastor has failed to connect with his essential underlying needs.

In her book *Beyond Deserving: Children, Parents, and Responsibility Revisited,* Dorothy Martyn discusses the "great open secret of responsibility." She writes that "acting out" is better used to refer to keeping subterranean matters from coming to the surface by "doing something" instead of becoming aware of those matters and thereby subjecting oneself to feeling something painful or unpleasant. In other words, "acting out" is a substitute for something else, and that something else consists of two activities. The first is to become acquainted with what is happening in one's cellar, so to speak, bringing it to the surface. The second, stemming from the first, is to allow the discernment and judgment of the conscious mind to consider an action before undertaking it.[20]

18. Dietrich Bonhoeffer, *Meditating on the Word* (Cambridge, Mass.: Cowley, 1986), 33.
19. Kornfeld, *Cultivating Wholeness,* 290.
20. Dorothy W. Martyn, *Beyond Deserving: Children, Parents, and Responsibility Revisited* (Grand Rapids: Eerdmans, 2007), 159.

"Subjecting oneself to feeling something painful or unpleasant" is precisely what the practice of self-connection enables one to do. One learns to acknowledge painful and unpleasant feelings; one faces shame, outrage, fear, jealousy, or helplessness in oneself and stays with these feelings long enough to discover the buried treasure hidden beneath them. The buried treasure is a bundle of unacknowledged yet precious needs that are clamoring for attention through the painful emotions.

In sexual acting out, the chronic unmet need is often for emotional intimacy. But if such intimacy is completely lacking in the pastor's life, *and if he is unaware of how much he longs for it,* he is vulnerable to *acting out* his desire rather than feeling the pain of his unmet need. By contrast, if he acknowledges his painful longing, he can then "allow the discernment and judgment of the conscious mind to consider" what kind of action he wants to undertake. Rather than "acting out" his feeling, in other words, he can *consciously connect* with the depth of his longing. If he can acknowledge the "beauty of this need" consciously, he will come to appreciate how much meaning, depth, joy, and delight emotional intimacy brings into most human lives. Only then can he decide what changes he might make to meet his need for intimacy in a way consonant with his values. To avoid burnout or sexual acting out, pastors and church leaders need not only a rich life of interpersonal fellowship but also skill in identifying and acting on behalf of their own needs.

Deepening Our Life of Prayer

NVC also offers tools for deepening *koinonia* with God through prayer. At the heart of Christian theology lies the presupposition that our most basic need is communion *(koinonia)* with God. As Christians, all our needs and values are deeply shaped by the gospel. Human beings are "not simply discrete units of personal need, but are what they are as they belong to an order of reality with certain ends."[21] From a Christian perspective, the order of reality to which they belong is the kingdom of God.

In intercessory prayer, the church calls upon the compassion of God as it has been revealed in Jesus Christ. The stories of Jesus' compassion

---

21. John Webster, "Response to 'What Wondrous Love Is This?'" in *For the Sake of the World: Karl Barth and the Future of Ecclesial Theology,* ed. George Hunsinger (Grand Rapids: Eerdmans, 2004), 163.

shape our imagination of God's compassion for the world. His feeding of thousands who were hungry, not only for bread, but for faith, hope, and love, helps us to see ourselves and our own needs among the hungry. His far-reaching compassion even toward those who crucified him gives us a glimpse of the immensity of divine love. When we open our hearts with compassion to any that suffer, we are thereby enabled by grace to participate in God's compassion for the world.[22] Our compassion, in other words, does not arise out of our own meager resources, but is grounded in God's own capacious suffering love. This theological grounding in God is critically important because human compassion is not large enough to meet the depth of another's true need. God alone can meet the need of the human heart. "Our hearts are restless until they rest in thee" (Saint Augustine).

In intercessory prayer, we listen to others with empathy and then intercede for them by giving voice to our understanding of their spirit's hunger before God.

Sometimes this entails "translating" their thoughts and judgments into their underlying needs. Consider this example:

Wife: [Referring to a physical therapist]. She's a bad therapist.
Nurse: *(listening empathically to what the wife is feeling and wanting)* Are you feeling annoyed and wanting to see a different quality of care?
Wife: She doesn't do anything. She made him stop walking when his pulse got high.
Nurse: *(continuing to hear the wife's feelings and wants)* Is it because you want your husband to get better that you're scared if the physical therapist doesn't push him, he won't get stronger?
Wife: *(starts to cry)* Yes, I'm so scared!
Nurse: Are you scared of losing him?
Wife: Yes, we've been together so long.
Nurse: *(listening for other feelings behind the fear)* Are you worrying about how you would feel if he dies?
Wife: I just can't imagine how I am going to live without him. He's always been there for me. Always.

---

22. Andrew Purves, *The Search for Compassion: Spirituality and Ministry* (Louisville: Westminster John Knox, 1989); see especially chap. 3: "The Wounded, Ministering God: A Theology of Divine Compassion," 60-81.

And later:

Wife: . . . I don't know how I am going to get through this alone. I haven't anyone . . . not even to talk to, except with you here . . . now. Even he won't talk about it. . . . Look at him! *(Husband remains silent and impassive).* He doesn't say anything!

Nurse: Are you sad, wishing the two of you could support each other and feel more connected?

Wife: Yes. *(She pauses, then makes a request)* Talk to him the way you talk to me.

Nurse: *(wishing to clearly understand the need that is being addressed behind the wife's request)* Are you wanting him to be listened to in a way that helps him express what he's feeling inside?

Wife: Yes, yes, that's exactly it![23]

Notice how the nurse basically ignores the wife's criticism and judgments, first of the physical therapist and then later of the husband. Instead she focuses entirely on what she hears as the wife's feelings and needs in this dire situation. Empathically putting herself into the woman's shoes, the nurse guesses that the woman is desperate for meaningful connection with her husband before he dies even though she lacks skill in giving voice to this desire. With the nurse's support, she is able to ask for help in talking with her husband in what may be the last conversation of their life together.

The nurse then goes on to draw out the husband in the same empathic way, listening for his needs with sensitivity and care. She quietly facilitates a conversation between husband and wife that enables them to share their love and grief as they are about to be parted from one another. Though the nurse in this example does not pray for the woman, the concrete help that she offers can be seen as an answer to the woman's unacknowledged prayer. The nurse's offer of help, in other words, can be interpreted as a sign that God has heard the woman's cry of anguish. Had the nurse desired to pray with her, she might have given explicit voice to the woman's longing for intimate connection with her husband. Expressing the longings of another's heart in intercessory prayer strengthens *koinonia* both vertically and horizontally. Such a prayer would enable the two to connect intimately with each other at the same time that they connect with God through prayer.

23. Marshall Rosenberg, *Nonviolent Communication: A Language of Life* (Encinitas, Calif.: PuddleDancer Press, 2003), 105-6.

Similarly, when we pray for ourselves, we search within for the un-expressed longings of our hearts. In other words, our prayer is deepened through our skill in identifying needs. Instead of going directly to our requests (all the things we long for God to "fix" in our lives), we meditate on the nature of our true need. The process of connecting with our needs is not a mechanical one, but rather a growing awareness of how all our needs are finally rooted and grounded in God. They are not in the end human qualities at all, but rather gifts of grace. "And my God will supply every need of yours according to his riches in glory in Christ Jesus" (Phil. 4:19). When we pray, we give voice in honest, vulnerable expression of our own heart's longing. Prayer connects us to God and to all the needs fulfilled in him.

The Christian image of the kingdom of God conveys the sense of "the beauty of needs," as qualities of being, better than anything I know of. The kingdom of God is a place overflowing with abundant life, goodness, and the fulfillment of every joy. The marriage feast of the Lamb evokes an image where human hunger, both physical and spiritual, is fulfilled. The lion and the lamb lie down together in peace. The rivers of righteousness flow down with a mighty roar. Justice and peace kiss. The hungry are fed; the lame leap for joy; those who were once in darkness now walk in the light. Unfathomable joy comes in that resurrection morning when God will wipe away every tear from our eyes. Thus when we seek to identify needs, our own or another's, we are engaging in a spiritual practice that leads to prayer. In prayer, we identify the specific needs motivating us in a particular situation, but all our needs point us to God and to our longing for God's kingdom to come on earth as it is in heaven.

Conclusion

Koinonia is both the origin and the telos of the church's existence. It is the goal of all our practices, and at the same time, it is something to be practiced. Nonviolent communication provides heightened awareness of the centrality of *koinonia* as well as skill in working toward it. It is especially helpful in situations when the peace and unity of our fellowship break down. When NVC is practiced as a spiritual discipline, members of the body of Christ will have practical tools for dealing constructively with criticism, for avoiding pastoral burnout or acting out, and for deepening the life of prayer. At more advanced levels, NVC can help church leaders to mediate conflict between parties, teach parents how to raise their children with love and respect, and promote real dialogue between parents and teens or husbands and wives. Leaders can help their parishioners heal from profound regret over choices they have made as well as find healing from past trauma.[24] Gifted practitioners can bring healing to whole communities in pain by helping them to hear one another's needs in situations of profound grief or estrangement. While these more complex applications of NVC lie beyond the scope of this chapter, even the most basic incorporation of NVC can deepen, sustain, and restore, again and again, our life together in the body of Christ until that day when our *koinonia* with God and each other is manifest in its fullness.

24. See Deborah van Deusen Hunsinger and Theresa F. Latini, *Transforming Church Conflict: Compassionate Leadership in Action* (Louisville: Westminster John Knox, 2013).

CHAPTER 7

Members of One Another

Building a Restorative Church

How is a community to heal when it learns of the sexual misconduct of its beloved pastor or of the treasurer's misappropriation of church funds? Or, where does a church turn for help when conflicts suddenly rage out of control? When shock, anger, or shame overwhelms a congregation, what steps will help the community regain its equilibrium? In the aftermath of churchwide trauma, how might congregational leaders sensitively open up communication about the painful ordeal?[1]

Church communities are often crippled for years, at times even destroyed, when they face such a shock to the system. Mobilizing their resources of intelligence, faith, and imagination, they are nevertheless unable to meet the overwhelming needs clamoring for their attention. As anxiety rises to a higher and higher pitch, individuals react from a feeling of personal threat rather than respond from a place of communal strength. The overriding need *to act together* as members of a common body gets lost in the chaotic emotions that arise.

When the entire church is reeling in pain, it can be difficult to invent structures and processes that will restore its equilibrium. Those congregations that have in place a restorative framework for responding to harm are best equipped to meet the challenges before them. This chapter seeks to introduce the concept of restorative practices as a promising avenue for responding to crisis, enduring conflict, harm, or community-wide trauma.

---

1. See the Web site for the Institute for Congregational Trauma and Growth at http://www.ictg.org/about.html. Its mission is to provide "research, education and networking tools for ministers, staffs and trained volunteers leading congregations and organizations after disaster."

Restorative practices (RP) is a transdisciplinary field of study that has grown during the past thirty years in various cultural contexts in response to complex community needs.[2] Though Christian theology has been a significant generative force in shaping fundamental norms in both theory and practice,[3] a restorative framework is little known and seldom adopted as an overarching structure for its explicit relational practice in contemporary churches. I believe that if restorative practices were more widely known, and its structures and processes more widely put into place, churches would be far better equipped to deal with conflict, harm, or trauma in a healthy manner. They might even be able to avoid the kind of entrenched conflict that not only causes emotional turmoil but also can provoke a crisis of faith. If the gulf between the preaching of the gospel and the actual relational practice of the congregation grows too wide, people are in danger not merely of cognitive dissonance, but of disillusionment, cynicism, or even loss of faith.

What Is Restorative Practices (RP)?

The International Institute of Restorative Practices offers a succinct definition:

2. Transdisciplinary studies are "projects that both integrate academic researchers from different unrelated disciplines and non-academic participants . . . to research a common goal and create new knowledge and theory. Transdisciplinarity combines interdisciplinarity with a participatory approach." See definitions of "disciplinary," "multidisciplinary," "participatory," "interdisciplinary," "transdisciplinary," and "integrative" studies in Bärbel Tress, Gunther Tress, Gary Fry, and Paul Opdam, eds., *From Landscape Research to Landscape Planning: Aspects of Integration, Education, and Application* (Dordrecht: Springer, 2006), 15-17.

3. Even in so-called secular venues, Christian values and norms are often either explicitly or implicitly present. See, for example, Desmond Tutu, *No Future without Forgiveness* (New York: Doubleday, 1999), which describes the work of the Truth and Reconciliation Commission in South Africa. Howard Zehr, a practicing Mennonite, is one of the "founding fathers" of restorative justice worldwide. See his books, *The Little Book of Restorative Justice* (Intercourse, Pa.: Good Books, 2002), and *Changing Lenses: A New Focus for Crime and Justice* (Scottdale, Pa.: Herald, 1990), among others. See also the work of John-Paul Lederach, a theorist and practitioner of transforming conflict at the level of international relations: *The Journey toward Reconciliation* (Scottdale, Pa.: Herald, 1999); *The Little Book of Conflict Transformation* (Intercourse, Pa.: Good Books, 2003); and *The Moral Imagination: The Art and Soul of Building Peace* (Oxford: Oxford University Press, 2010), among others.

The social science of restorative practices is an emerging field of study that enables people to restore and build community in an increasingly disconnected world. It offers a common thread to tie together theory, research and practice in seemingly disparate fields, such as education, counseling, criminal justice, social work and organizational management.

... Restorative practices is the study of building social capital and achieving social discipline through participatory learning and decision-making.[4]

Scholars from the disparate fields engaged in this area of study approach it from a wide variety of theoretical perspectives, drawn from their own academic disciplines and the specific needs of their cultural and social contexts. What unites the various disciplines and experienced practitioners in this field of study is a commitment (developed both theoretically and practically) to working *with* people in order to deepen community ties instead of doing things *to* them or *for* them (or alternatively, not doing anything at all). "The fundamental premise of restorative practices is that people are happier, more cooperative and productive, and more likely to make positive changes when those in authority do things *with* them, rather than *to* them or *for* them."[5]

Consider the following chart.[6] A restorative approach is portrayed in the upper-right-hand quadrant as that relational stance that sets high expectations for behavior at the same time it offers high levels of support. None of the other options (FOR, NOT, and TO) reinforce the kinds of relational patterns that support people in taking responsibility for themselves. The upper right quadrant that features the word "WITH" describes a relational style that is respected by others because it is authoritative without being authoritarian. (The adjectives at the bottom of each

---

4. See http://www.iirp.edu/whatisrp.php. Note the use of the term "restorative practices" (in the plural) in this definition. Some theorists prefer to speak of "restorative practice" (in the singular) to indicate their understanding that RP is not a set of techniques or processes, but rather is an overarching framework for understanding and strengthening relationship, a way of thinking and being. Within that framework, many kinds of processes or practices may be usefully employed. I am indebted to Mark Vander Vennen of FaithCARE for this point. See www.shalemnetwork.org.

5. http://www.iirp.edu/whatisrp.php.

6. Social Discipline Window, created by Paul McCold and Ted Wachtel, 2000. http://www.iirp.edu/pdf/paradigm.pdf.

Response Styles

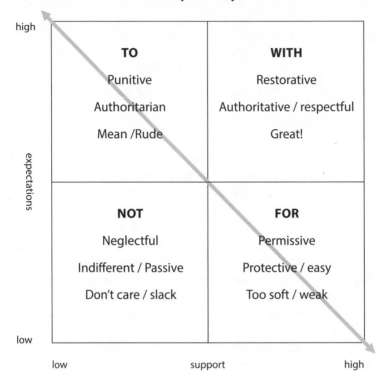

(an adaptation of the Social Discipline Window, by Paul McCold and Ted Wachtel, 2000)

quadrant reflect student evaluations of teachers whose relational styles are described there. Students are respectful toward those in authority who first of all respect *them* by taking their needs into account when making decisions that affect their lives.) But the word "WITH" also entails an acknowledgment by those in authority that they genuinely *do not know* in any particular instance what is needed to restore a sense of well-being to the community. The community decides together how to live out its values. Those "in authority" do not own the process; the community as a whole owns it.

People need to be included in decisions that matter to them. They need to have their core values heard and their perspectives considered.

As members of an interdependent society, all persons need avenues by which they can contribute to the community to which they belong.[7] This becomes even more significant when the community is in pain because of some harm done. In a healthy community, individuals are able both to give of themselves and to perceive their impact on others as well as receive from others and gratefully acknowledge them in turn. A profound sense of mutuality is thus embedded in the single word "with."[8] At the heart of this transdisciplinary field, in both theory and practice, lies a commitment not to use one's power *over* others, but to engage as much as possible in relationships of mutuality for the sake of building interdependent community. Such a commitment can be challenging to sustain in the context of coercive structures that are intrinsic to many societal institutions.

Members of One Another

Typical of contemporary discourse, what was once woven together as a seamless whole — one's theological assumptions, ethics, and practice — has now been fragmented into disparate avenues of inquiry. As members of a multicultural and multifaith society, we cannot suppose that others will share our theological assumptions. It is important, therefore, to differentiate two interdependent aims. I believe that as Christians, our deepest loyalty and most enduring commitment are to Jesus Christ and to all that we have received by faith in him. As we root and ground ourselves in Christ's love, we will seek to articulate a set of beliefs and engage in con-

7. In his book *Nonviolent Communication: A Language of Life* (Encinitas, Calif.: PuddleDancer Press, 2003), Marshall Rosenberg argues that *contribution* and *belonging* are fundamental, universal human needs.

8. In his article "Reconceiving Practice," Craig Dykstra argues that a modern understanding of "practices" is "ahistorical, individualistic, and technological, something done *to* and *for* others, undergirded by a utilitarian ethic. By contrast, he argues that the practices of the Christian faith are more adequately conceived as being cooperative and communal 'complex traditions of interaction,' something we do *with* others. We learn the practices of Christian faith by participating in them in the community, through mentoring relationships with others who are competent 'practitioners.' By entering into the practices of the faith, we develop new knowledge and insight that otherwise cannot be gained." Deborah van Deusen Hunsinger, *Pray without Ceasing: Revitalizing Pastoral Care* (Grand Rapids: Eerdmans, 1995), xi. See Dykstra, "Reconceiving Practice," in *Shifting Boundaries: Contextual Approaches to the Structure of Theological Education,* ed. Barbara Wheeler and Edward Farley (Louisville: Westminster John Knox, 1991).

crete practices that grow out of our calling to Christian discipleship. At the same time, as we pursue our mission in the wider world, we will seek ways to join forces with persons of other faiths (or no faith) who desire to build and restore community ties on the basis of fundamental shared values. As Glen Stassen comments, "In public discourse, in a pluralistic society, we need *both* (1) an *explicitly Christian ethic* with a strong scriptural base and (2) a *public ethic* that appeals to reason, experience, and need and that cannot place the same emphasis on Scripture and prayer that an explicitly Christian ethic can."[9] In community-wide conflicts or in tragedies of national or international significance, when we seek to join forces with those outside the church, we will appeal to shared values such as compassion and mutual respect or to universal norms such as justice and peace. But within the Christian community, in order to articulate our fundamental beliefs and values, we will seek to make explicit the scriptural base and theological norms by which we orient ourselves.

The church, though to the eye perhaps just as fragmented as the world around it, is known by faith to be a single body by virtue of each member's participation in Christ. Because all are members of Christ's body, all are also members of one another.

> For just as the body is one and has many members, and all the members of the body, though many, are one body, so it is with Christ. For by one Spirit we were all baptized into one body — Jews or Greeks, slaves or free — and all were made to drink of one Spirit. For the body does not consist of one member but of many. If the foot should say, "Because I am not a hand, I do not belong to the body," that would not make it any less a part of the body. And if the ear should say, "Because I am not an eye, I do not belong to the body," that would not make it any less a part of the body. If the whole body were an eye, where would be the hearing? If the whole body were an ear, where would be the sense of smell? But as it is, God arranged the organs in the body, each one of them, as he chose. If all were a single organ, where would the body be? As it is, there are many parts, yet one body. The eye cannot say to the hand, "I have no need of you," nor again the head to the feet, "I have no need of you." On the contrary, the parts of the body which seem to be weaker are indispensable. (1 Cor. 12:12-22)

9. Glen H. Stassen, *Just Peacemaking: Transforming Initiatives for Justice and Peace* (Louisville: Westminster John Knox, 1992), 93-94.

Is an eye more important to the functioning of the body than an ear? Doesn't a body function best when it has not only eyes, but also ears, not only a sense of smell, but also hands and feet? Even if the feet do their part, how can the body function without hands as well? Doesn't the body depend upon each member to bring its unique gifts and capacities to the whole? How could the body function if only one kind of faculty were present? Even the weakest member is indispensable.

Each one's essential indispensability is affirmed, as Paul sets forth his understanding of the radical interdependence of the members of the church. While the indispensability of some may not be obvious to general perception, those who walk by faith know that each person has a unique place of belonging by virtue of the person's participation in Christ. Moreover, because we internalize the context in which we live, what is outside of us is also inside each of us. We literally cannot cut ourselves off from the body to which we belong. "If one member suffers, all suffer together" (1 Cor. 12:26). The suffering of one member, however seemingly marginal, does in fact affect the entire body.

The premise, that the suffering of one brings suffering to the whole body, functions, I believe, as a basic presupposition of restorative practices, though it is often cut loose from its moorings in Christian theology. Seldom made explicit, it is nevertheless crucial for understanding the core values of restorative practices, no matter what the context.[10]

Conflicts in the Church

Conflicts in the church are hardly new. We have only to recall the apostle Paul's intense frustration with the church at Corinth. Loyalties that divided the church into factions were intolerable. He reminded them repeatedly

---

10. Various cultures and religions have their own conceptualizations of the essential interdependence of persons. Buddhist monk Thich Nhat Hanh, as mentioned in chapter 2, speaks of human "interbeing"; Bishop Desmond Tutu speaks of *ubuntu;* and many Christians understand *koinonia* with God and one another as the telos of human life: partnership, communion, or mutual indwelling. Consider this description of *ubuntu* by Tutu: "*Ubuntu* is very difficult to render into a Western language. It speaks of the very essence of being human. . . . It is to say, 'My humanity is caught up, is inextricably bound up, in yours.' We belong in a bundle of life. We say, 'A person is a person through other persons.' It is not, 'I think therefore I am.' It says rather: 'I am human because I belong. I participate. I share.'" Desmond Tutu, *No Future without Forgiveness* (New York: Doubleday, 1999), 31.

of their unity in Christ. "What I mean is that each one of you says, 'I belong to Paul,' or 'I belong to Apollos,' or 'I belong to Cephas,' or 'I belong to Christ'" (1 Cor. 1:12). Paul sees distorted theology at the root of such division — "Is Christ divided? Was Paul crucified for you? Or were you baptized in the name of Paul?" (1:13) — which he seeks to correct. The community's central identity as members of Christ's own body, and therefore as members one of another, is his basic presupposition. An appeal to our underlying unity in Christ perhaps remains the most persuasive argument that might still inspire a congregation to listen to one another with patience. The deeper the congregation's devotion to Christ, the greater will be its willingness to bear with one another, even in those situations when it is weary with conflict or stunned by crisis. What, apart from Jesus Christ himself, can inspire the members to reach toward those with whom they disagree?

In recent years, contemporary students of congregational dynamics have been able to shed helpful light on the specific features of such a factionalized community.[11] In some conflicted churches, secrets distort information, creating alienation for some and a false sense of companionship for others, thereby raising the level of anxiety system-wide. Keeping secrets seriously divides a family or community. Those who are "in" on the secret are able to communicate with one another far better than with anyone outside the group, "*about any issue,* not just about the secret."[12] The most important impact of secrets on the community's emotional well-being, however, is that "they exacerbate other pathological processes unrelated to the content of the particular secret, because secrets generally function to keep anxiety at higher energy levels. . . . The formation of a . . . secret is always symptomatic of other things going on in the [community]."[13] Other pathological processes include key members cutting themselves off from the community for a while, whose departure from the community intensifies the anxiety of those who remain. Communication becomes indirect as attempts are made to avoid the emotional minefields created by taboo subjects. Congregational culture grows more conflict-avoidant. Triangles form. The anxiety arising between any two parties is absorbed by a third party who listens to both but is powerless to resolve their differences unless or until she finds

---

11. See Deborah van Deusen Hunsinger and Theresa F. Latini, *Transforming Church Conflict: Compassionate Leadership in Action* (Louisville: Westminster John Knox, 2013).

12. Edwin Friedman, *Generation to Generation: Family Process in Church and Synagogue* (New York: Guilford Press, 1985), 52.

13. Friedman, *Generation to Generation,* 53.

a way to become a connecting bridge between them.[14] True impasses, in which members no longer recall the real issues, may evolve. The conflict ceases to be about the issues and begins to be about persons instead. Labeling, scapegoating, and diagnosing others prevail.[15] Power is no longer shared but is used by one group at the expense of another. Decision-making structures are altered to reinforce the power of the ruling faction.

The sense of alienation and hopelessness that typically grows out of long-term, unresolved conflict is among its most destructive fruit. As persons shrink back from engaging in overt conflict, it becomes more and more difficult to assess the complex dynamics at work. Typically, many disparate conflicts have arisen over time with various people involved. One person may see himself as the victim of another's hurtful action, while the other would identify *him* as the offender, focusing not on that action, but on the one immediately preceding it, to which she is simply responding. It is often challenging for church leaders to identify *a specific action* that might become the focus of a fruitful conversation. What is the conflict *about?* How might a particular focus be found that will open up channels of communication about what is at stake? If the aims of a restorative paradigm are mutual understanding, self-responsibility, and fruitful action (and not mutual blame, self-justification, or finding a scapegoat), then in a certain sense it doesn't matter what the chosen focus is. What particular focus might best assist the church in reversing negative spirals toward isolation and help facilitate connection among its members?

Conflicts in a community are like mushrooms in a forest, which seem to sprout up at random. Though a professional mycologist would recognize the many mushrooms as a single rhizome (the horizontal root stem), the ordinary observer sees only a multitude of individual mushrooms. When persons are members of one another, as they are in the church, any problem usually conceals an underlying root conflict that is larger and more

---

14. "When any two parts of a system become uncomfortable with one another, they will 'triangle in' or focus upon a third person, or issue, as a way of stabilizing their own relationship with one another." Friedman later reflects that though "the most triangled person in any set of relationships is always the most vulnerable; when the laws of emotional triangles are understood . . . [the triangled party] tends to become the most powerful." Friedman, *Generation to Generation,* 35-39.

15. K. Brynolf Lyon, "Scapegoating in Congregational and Group Life: Practical Theological Reflections on the Unbearable," in *Healing Wisdom: Depth Psychology and the Pastoral Ministry,* ed. Kathleen Greider, Deborah van Deusen Hunsinger, and Felicity Brock Kelcourse (Grand Rapids: Eerdmans, 2010), 141-56.

complex than any lone individual can perceive. How do the members of the community conceive of the overall shape of the rhizome hidden from view? The complex root system can be described adequately only through multiple perspectives. An intentional restorative process is designed to understand the *meaning* each person makes of the root conflict, and not to determine "what *really* happened."[16] Just as each of the four Gospel writers understood the meaning of Jesus' life, death, and resurrection differently, so every member of the community will make unique meaning out of the turmoil the church is experiencing.

To set up a churchwide restorative process, it is necessary only to choose a single manifestation of the complex underlying conflict, trusting that any entry point will lead to the root. With the careful listening of those who gather for a restorative circle, any particular focus would enable a sustained meditation on the interrelated parts of a single conflict, in both its unity and its complexity. By intentionally choosing a single focus, in other words, the intricately woven interdependence of the community will be disclosed. Though the whole is hidden in any part (i.e., any particular mushroom will lead to the hidden root system), it is helpful to choose a specific focus that will likely be significant for the community as a whole.

Churches that embrace a restorative paradigm understand that healthy open conflict is far less destructive than denied or suppressed conflict; in fact, open conflict can bring a community new vitality:

> Productive conflict can include a feeling of change, expansion, joy. It may at times have to involve anguish and pain too; but even these are different from the feelings involved in destructive or blocked conflict. Destructive conflict calls forth the conviction that one cannot possibly "win" or, more accurately, that nothing can really change or enlarge. It often involves a feeling that one must move away from one's deeply felt motives, that one is losing the connection with one's most importantly held desires and needs. . . . Adults have been well schooled in suppressing conflict but not in conducting constructive conflict. Adults don't seem to know how to enter into it with integrity and respect and with some degree of confidence and hope.[17]

16. The single rhizome of the mushroom plant as an extended metaphor to describe conflict in community was developed by Dominic Barter in his workshop "Building Compassionate Justice for 21st Century," October 2008, in St. Paul, Minn.

17. Jean Baker Miller, *Toward a New Psychology of Women* (Boston: Beacon Press, 1976), 129.

Churches that adopt a restorative practice framework will not be conflict-avoidant. These churches will teach their members how to initiate constructive conflict with some degree of confidence and hope.[18] As members work through conflicts successfully, they will increase not only their skill level but also their trust in the process.

Conflicts of many kinds and at various levels of intensity need sensitive, differentiated responses. Consider this continuum of increasing levels of conflict:[19]

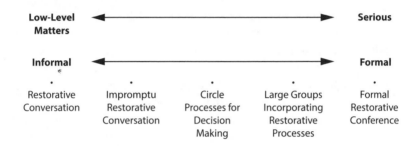

Low-Level Matters				Serious
Informal				Formal
Restorative Conversation	Impromptu Restorative Conversation	Circle Processes for Decision Making	Large Groups Incorporating Restorative Processes	Formal Restorative Conference

When hurt occurs in the context of a solid relationship of trust, it can usually be addressed by simple affective statements (at the far left of the continuum). An example might be a parishioner saying to his pastor, "I felt hurt that you didn't return my phone call last week when you heard that my daughter was seriously ill. I especially needed your support at such a stressful time." Such an honest expression of one's feelings and needs would likely evoke a response that would help restore trust and contribute to mutual understanding.[20] As we move toward the right of the continuum, we find conflicts of a more serious nature that require more stable structures.[21] An impromptu restorative conversation might be undertaken by

18. Interpersonal skills in nonviolent communication can be and are being taught in a variety of contexts, including Christian churches. See Rosenberg, *Nonviolent Communication,* and Hunsinger and Latini, *Transforming Church Conflict.*

19. International Institute of Restorative Practices Canada, developed by Bruce Schenk, presented at the IIRP International Conference, Bethlehem, Pa., October 2010.

20. Nonviolent communication teaches that expressing one's feelings and needs, instead of judgments, evaluations, or diagnoses, helps to restore connection among individuals and groups. See Rosenberg, *Nonviolent Communication.*

21. See Conflict Intensity Chart: A Resource for Committees on Ministry, PC(USA), with its description of five levels of increasing conflict, based on the work of Rev. Speed Leas, *Moving Your Church through Conflict* (Bethesda, Md.: Alban Institute, 1985). Available online.

two or three people who understand that the purpose of the conversation is to promote mutual understanding. Those who have been instructed by Matthew 18 will recognize the progression: first, try to work things out directly with the other person involved. If you are unable to resolve matters at that (lowest) level, then ask one or two others to join you.

> "If another member of the church sins against you, go and point out the fault when the two of you are alone. If the member *listens to you,* you have regained that one. But if you are *not listened to,* take one or two others along with you, so that every word may be confirmed by the evidence of two or three witnesses. If the member *refuses to listen to them,* tell it to the church; and if the offender *refuses to listen* even to the church, let such a one be to you as a Gentile and a tax collector. Truly I tell you, whatever you bind on earth will be bound in heaven, and whatever you loose on earth will be loosed in heaven. Again, truly I tell you, if two of you agree on earth about anything you ask, it will be done for you by my Father in heaven. For where two or three are gathered in my name, I am there among them." (Matt. 18:15-20 NRSV, emphasis added)

Congregations need instruction in resolving harm at these lower levels in order to prevent conflicts from escalating. At this level, participants who have been trained to listen — *note the key skill of listening* repeated four times — will generally be confident that though the conversation may be difficult, it will be worthwhile in the end. Those churches that have held circles for a wide variety of purposes will have all the mechanisms in place, as well as a considerable fund of trust, for tackling the more difficult large-group or churchwide restorative circles.

Circles for decision making are quite different — both in intent and in process — from a typical church meeting in which the pros and cons of a possible course of action are debated and a "majority rules" vote is taken. Restorative circles are not designed to be forums for winning proponents, persuading others to one's point of view, or making an opposing party look bad. Such tactics only increase ill feeling and lead to polarization. A restorative approach *encourages* those the majority disagrees with to speak up, not so they can be defeated, but so that their needs can be fully heard and taken to heart. A restorative church knows that if it operates within a win/lose paradigm, the whole church will lose. Just as in a marriage where only win/win arguments enable the couple to flourish, so also in a church, members are careful *not* to try to "win" at someone else's expense. As we move further toward the far right-hand column to large-group restorative processes or to a churchwide formal restorative conference, clear structures and processes need to be in place that will provide safety for more challenging conversations. Though these conversations can sometimes be painful, they often issue in newfound energy and even joy. As members speak of their deepest convictions, they grow in respect and understanding of one another. Their unity in Christ becomes more visible as they see that those with whom they disagree are taking their views to heart and considering them in a new light.

At the formal conference end of the continuum, it can be helpful to invite an outside facilitator to oversee the process.[22] Many situations arise in the church where a pastor needs to be an active participant in the circle, and not the facilitator. Including the pastor as a member of the circle enables members to understand the pastor as a human being with feelings and needs and not simply as the person in authority. Dominic Barter tells the story of a kindergartner who requested a restorative circle over an upsetting event at her school. The principal participated in the circle as an equal partner to help restore harmony.[23]

It is in the context of community conflict — when one member of the church is sinning against another and *refuses to hear* the impact it has on others — that Jesus explicitly promises to be in their midst. The promise of Jesus' presence is given to us precisely in those situations in which we feel most threatened, when we have been hurt and find ourselves unable to make our voice heard. When one who "has sinned against us" *refuses* to listen to us, we are instructed to ask one or two others to go with us to find a way to restore trust (impromptu restorative conversation). Skill in listening is essential for such a conversation to succeed. If the person refuses to hear the impact of his actions on others, conversations that include still others may need to take place. Because any particular offense is nested in larger complex processes, the perspective of others will widen the scope, helping to shed light on the overarching context. When the community's clear intent is one of mutual understanding and not blaming or scapegoating, the circle process can be liberating and exciting. New information will emerge;

22. FaithCARE in Hamilton, Canada, for example, provides consultation for churches in crisis, using a restorative practice framework. See www.shalemnetwork.org.

23. Barter, "Building Compassionate Justice for 21st Century."

hearts closed down and hardened will open up and soften; and creative new directions will spring up.

What if the person who has brought suffering to the body refuses to listen to the whole church? Jesus says such a person is to be treated as a Gentile or a tax collector. Churches through the ages have taken Jesus to mean that such a person is to be utterly rejected, perhaps even cast out from the community. Yet here we must ask about Jesus' own practice toward Gentiles and tax collectors. Does he refuse to have anything to do with them? *No, he seeks deepened fellowship with them.*[24] He invites himself into the home of Zacchaeus, the despised tax collector, for example, and engages in serious theological conversation with the woman from Samaria.[25] Against all the customs of his culture, Jesus listens to those that others consider sinful and unworthy. Even at the formal conference end of the continuum, when clear harm has been done, the goal is not to cast out those who have harmed others, but to deepen fellowship with them so that a true communion of mutual understanding can grow.

Guiding Principles of Restorative Practice

When strife or trauma has come to the community, the fundamental questions informing a restorative approach would be:

1. Who has been hurt?
2. What are their needs?
3. Whose obligations are these?
4. Who has a stake in this situation?
5. What is the appropriate process to involve stakeholders to put things right?[26]

The focus of the work is to identify and address the needs of every person impacted by the incident, *including* those who have caused harm. Recognizing our own need for mercy, we are to extend mercy toward any who acknowledge their responsibility for their choices. If a clear restorative

24. Lederach, *The Journey toward Reconciliation*, 134.
25. Though Samaritans were not technically Gentiles, "Jews have no dealings with Samaritans" (John 4:9).
26. Zehr, *The Little Book*, 38.

process has already been established in the church, parishioners will expect a restorative circle to be called, so that the matter can be discussed in a safe and productive manner. It is crucial that the person who has brought harm to the community acknowledges the *fact* of her actions. The *meaning* of the action for her, as well as for others, will come out in the restorative circle. Not only will others come to understand her motivations for acting as she did, but she will have an opportunity to hear the impact her choices had on other members of the community.

Guiding principles at work in a restorative paradigm are listed below:

1. The conflict or difficulty, whatever its dimensions, belongs to the community in which it takes place. It needs to be owned by the community and not taken over by outside agents (e.g., the criminal justice system, social workers, lawyers or other authorities, professionals, or agencies attempting to offer support).[27]
2. Its purpose (and central focus) is to restore and heal relationships through face-to-face participation of those affected.
3. It is a voluntary process for everyone involved. No coercion of any kind is used. People are invited to participate, not mandated to do so.
4. Trained facilitators from within the community coordinate the restorative processes.
5. Each person participating will have equal access to the processes developed as well as informed consent upon which to make a decision whether to participate or not.
6. Restorative circles end in an action plan to which everyone agrees. Those directly affected together determine the outcome.
7. No observers are included in the process, only participants who have a vital stake in the outcome.
8. Everyone present is given a chance to speak and be heard.
9. The greater the alignment with these principles, the more restorative the outcome.[28]

---

27. Nils Christie argues this thesis in his groundbreaking article, "Conflicts as Property": "My suspicion is that criminology to some extent has amplified a process where conflicts have been taken away from the parties directly involved and thereby have either disappeared or become other people's property. In both cases a deplorable outcome." "Conflicts as Property," *British Journal of Criminology* 17, no. 1 (January 1977): 1.

28. These principles represent my understanding of the teachings of Dominic Barter at the New York Intensive Residential Training in Nonviolent Communication in Binghamton, N.Y., August 2008.

Participants in the circle decide what strategies might best serve the needs of the whole by discovering which specific actions will be done, by whom, and by what date. Participants then make requests of one another or suggest constructive actions that either directly meet the identified needs or symbolically connect to them in a meaningful way.

Choosing a Planning Team

In any serious conflict in the church, it is important to create a planning team or "reference committee."[29] Such a team is made up of lay leaders who are familiar not only with the issues the congregation is facing but also with the history of some of its long-standing interpersonal impasses. These leaders need to be sanctioned by the church governing body and widely respected by the congregation. If church factions are polarized, it is important to have proponents of each faction on the team. It would be unwise, however, to choose extreme representatives of one party or another. It is best to choose those more moderate in their opinions, especially if they are skilled in listening to those with whom they disagree. Their success in offering effective leadership will depend in large part on their ability to work together as a team. The quality of their dialogue "tends to affect the quality of the overall dialogue within the congregation. . . . Their essential job is to advocate a fair process and not a particular outcome."[30]

The planning team will oversee a process that has three segments: a *precircle* to support clarity about the specific act that will serve as the focal point for conversation and to explain the whole process to those who need to be included; a *restorative circle* that aims toward mutual understanding, self-responsibility, and effective action; and a *postcircle* to help the community assess the level of satisfaction with the steps taken. Restorative circles can function at varying degrees of complexity and varying levels of emotional intensity. In each case, only those people directly or indirectly impacted by the act should be involved. Because of the complex interdependent nature of a church community or in the event of a serious crisis, situations may arise in which a churchwide restorative circle is needed.

29. "Forming a Reference Committee in Congregational Change or Conflict," in David R. Brubaker, *Promise and Peril: Understanding and Managing Change and Conflict in Congregations* (Herndon, Va.: Alban Institute, 2009), 147-50.

30. Brubaker, *Promise and Peril,* 149.

This kind of circle is represented on the restorative practice continuum at the far right: *Formal Restorative Conference.* If the church is familiar with a restorative approach, having worked frequently at much lower levels of conflict or crisis, the planning team can go into immediate action.

Churches dealing with any specific action that has diminished the community's sense of well-being gather to talk about the harm that has impacted them, by answering a series of prepared questions (that will be contextualized for the specific situation). At the most generalized level, each person will be asked to reflect on three questions:

- What do you want others to know about how you are now in relation to [what happened]? What impact has this event had on you? *(Grounding in the present — this seeks to support mutual understanding.)*
- What do you want others to know about what you were looking for when you acted (or responded) as you did to the event? *(Investigating the past — this seeks to support self-responsibility.)*
- What would you like to see happen next? Is there a specific request or offer you want to make that would address the needs of the community as you understand it? *(Agreeing to future action — this seeks to support effective movement forward.)*[31]

Each person in the circle will have an opportunity to speak and to be heard. Questions that first ground the participants in the present help build bridges of mutual understanding. Questions that investigate the reasons people chose to respond as they did help each person to take responsibility for his choices. And requests or offers of support that are concrete and doable help promote effective action. Situations that interface with legal processes (such as the sexual misconduct of the pastor or the treasurer's

---

31. The forms of these questions are based on my understanding of Dominic Barter's creative work with restorative circles in Brazil. Formal restorative conferences (or circles) take on different shapes depending on their institutional context and their specific purpose. For example, family group conferencing might occur in the context of making foster-care decisions in family and youth social services. The criminal justice system has formal procedures for helping courts to determine sentences based on victim-impact statements developed by communities that have been harmed. Schools hold restorative conferences to deal with delinquencies and disruptions in classes, either in a particular classroom or, if the whole school has been impacted, schoolwide. In each instance, the questions asked and considered by the participants will vary according to the specific needs of those involved, but it is important to address the present, the past, and the future, giving everyone a chance to be heard.

misappropriation of church funds) will need clear guidelines that respect the rights of the alleged offender and victims, but at the same time attend to the congregation's needs for healing and connection at a time of potentially overwhelming stress.[32]

Structuring a Churchwide Restorative Circle

A churchwide restorative circle can transform conflict in completely unexpected ways.[33] There is a natural flow to conflict that needs assistance in reaching its full potential. Ideally, two facilitators (or one, if necessary) help the group establish clear guidelines and keep the process on track. The facilitators' tasks are:

- to help the community come to an agreement about guidelines for the dialogue by explaining the overall aims of the restorative circle;
- to check whether each person who speaks is heard to her own satisfaction;
- to prepare each participant in a precircle process before the circle meets (precircles will be explained below);
- to schedule the date and time of the restorative circle;
- to choose a quiet and symbolically meaningful place for the circle, and to have drinks, tissues, pens, and paper available;
- to set forth the process clearly for all participants; and
- to greet all persons as they enter the space, initiate a simple process for introductions to be made, and offer a clear opening sentence that reminds them of the intention that brought them all there.[34]

The group's first task will be to develop process guidelines. These typically include showing respect for each person by agreeing to keep what is said within the group (agreement regarding confidentiality), and by having only one person speak at a time (agreement regarding respect and fair-

32. For restorative justice guidelines in victim/offender situations, see Terry O'Connell's groundbreaking work at www.realjustice.org.

33. For practical ideas and useful suggestions for setting up such circles, see Ron Kraybill, *The Little Book of Cool Tools for Hot Topics: Group Tools to Facilitate Meetings When Things Are Hot* (Intercourse, Pa.: Good Books, 2007).

34. I am drawing here on my understanding of the key elements required of facilitators as presented by Dominic Barter in his workshop "Building Compassionate Justice for 21st Century."

ness) — sometimes facilitated by the use of a "talking piece" or symbolic object that is held by the person who is speaking.[35]

Setting chairs in a circle communicates a commitment to valuing every person's voice. As Kay Pranis comments, a circle communicates, by its very shape, that "no person is more important than anyone else."[36] The focus of the meeting should be described in neutral terms to avoid attributing blame to any particular person or persons. Whatever happened is an event that cries out for understanding. The aim of calling a circle is to facilitate a greater sense of connection among the members of the community, giving each member a keen sense of belonging. If a harmful event involves an actual crime, the legal process might need to occur concomitantly with the circle process. It is crucial in such cases to distinguish between such procedures and the congregation's urgent need for care and healing. Fears about legal ramifications will sometimes muzzle a congregation at the very time they most need to hear from one another. If discord has arisen in the body, the group must have a safe way to come together and process the emotions that are having such an impact.

The core aim of a restorative circle is to facilitate connection among its members through mutual understanding, self-responsibility, and an action plan.[37] Mutual understanding is supported when each person has an opportunity to be heard about the *significance* of a particular event, the meaning that it holds for him now. After each person speaks, the facilitator asks one of the members of the circle, "What did you hear that is important to him?" That member replies with a summary of the essence of what he heard. Then the facilitator turns to the original speaker and asks, "Is that what you wanted understood?" By adding this simple step, everyone in the circle receives immediate feedback about how he has been heard. This gives each person an opportunity to restate what he wants to be known by others until he is heard completely to his satisfaction. This back-and-forth

35. "The use of a talking piece allows for full expression of emotions, deeper listening, thoughtful reflection, and an unhurried pace." Kay Pranis, *The Little Book of Circle Processes: A New/Old Approach to Peacemaking* (Intercourse, Pa.: Good Books, 2005), 12.

36. Pranis, *The Little Book*, 8.

37. I am indebted to Dominic Barter's oral presentations in which he teaches the processes, principles, and structures of restorative circles. Barter, a certified trainer in nonviolent communication, is an internationally recognized facilitator and teacher of restorative practices. See his Web site for information on his work in Brazil and his teaching throughout the world. My understanding of his teachings has been contextualized specifically for the church. http://www.restorativecircles.org/.

dialogue between speaker and listener seems to slow down the process. In the end, it brings much more ease to the process because little facilitates mutual understanding more readily than the experience of being heard as one hopes to be heard.

The intention of this process is to focus on the people present and how they see and understand one another, in order to reestablish a sense of connection. The facilitation helps the participants to gain trust in the process as well as insight about other members of the community who are affected by an important event in the church's life. Sometimes the process may involve the gathering of the entire community, and several circles may need to be held. Hearing from others in this way helps to build bridges of mutual understanding as each person begins to hear the others' humanity.

Self-responsibility takes place when each person in the community acknowledges and owns the choices she has made about the act or event in question, by engaging this question: "What do you want others to know about what you were looking for when you acted as you did?" Every member of the congregation has contributed to the ethos of the community by her actions (or inaction). Each person is encouraged to reflect on what in particular she was seeking in relation to the act. As each person hears from others, she may be able to give more articulate voice to her own motivations (i.e., what needs she was trying to meet through her particular choices). Naming these before the community helps persons to take responsibility for their own needs, a process that at once decreases blame and increases a sense of empowerment.

Because the process is slow and reflective, giving people the time and space to process their emotions and taking the time for full reflective listening, a sturdy bridge among the participants is built. Only after the interpersonal bridge is securely in place do the facilitators move the process to the third step: the creation of an action plan. With restorative circles, churches can avoid the common mistake of rushing into action. After a trauma or tragedy, many people will offer some version of the advice that was a popular slogan in the 1960s: "Don't mourn, organize!" While taking action often brings with it a wonderful sense of empowerment, it will not accomplish a fraction of what it is meant to accomplish if the step of *mourning together* is sidestepped. When the members of the community are reconnected with each other from the heart, a palpable shift can be felt in the room. At that point, the third question can be asked: "What would you like to see happen next? Is there a specific request — or offer — that you want to make that would address the needs of the community, as you understand them?"

At this point in the conversation, creative strategies usually begin to flow, sometimes to overflow. The group is energized by the hard work it has done in steps 1 and 2 and is eager to move forward together in a constructive way. Any offering or request needs to be concrete, specific, and doable within a particular time frame. The action plan aims to take into consideration *all* the needs that have been expressed. Here an exciting sense of collaboration often grows palpably. A plan is agreed upon by all members of the circle and is to be carried out within a specific period of time. At the end of the whole process (*after* the action plan has been implemented), a postcircle will be called to assess whether the action plan did in fact meet the needs of the community as it had hoped. If not, a new action plan can be created.

It is not the responsibility of the facilitators to resolve the conflict; this is the work of the entire community. The facilitators enter the circle process, along with everyone else, *not knowing* how things will go. They do not have a specific end in mind. Holding fast to the fundamental principles of the practice, facilitators work throughout the entire process *with* the community, and in many instances are themselves members of the community. They do not enter the circle holding on to roles of authority but join the circle simply as those members who will guard the integrity of the process and assist the group in adhering to the agreed-upon principles. Because restorative circles are completely voluntary, the persons who commit themselves to the circle process are those willing to take responsibility for the next steps. Anyone who does not wish to take part is free to decline. In that case, however, the facilitators make it clear that the circle will proceed without them. In this way, no one has the power to sabotage the healing of the community by choosing not to participate.

Precircles

As mentioned, there are three distinct phases to the overall process for a churchwide restorative conference: precircles, the restorative circle itself, and the postcircle. The facilitators meet with each group (or each individual, depending on the scope and the particulars of the event to be discussed) represented in a precircle meeting. That is to say, the facilitators meet with the authors of the act, the direct recipients, and the larger community (those indirectly impacted) in three different precircles. The facilitators' goals in these precircles are to forge an empathic connection with each person involved; to gain clarity about the precise nature of the act by asking each person "what happened" as that person sees it; to ask who needs to be involved to resolve the conflict; and to gain each individual's informed consent. The facilitators lay out the purpose of the circle, the precise questions that will be asked, and the underlying principles that will be adhered to. The overall process is explained.

The facilitators end the precircles by asking each person whether he would like to participate. Their aim is to adapt the form to the local context and culture as much as possible so that it will truly serve the people involved. As they help the congregants to articulate what really matters to them about the incident, the facilitators show forth a collaborative spirit that helps to form a sturdy bond of trust. As more people decide to participate, it becomes more promising that the circle(s) will reach its restorative aim.

Postcircles

A postcircle is called by the facilitators at an agreed-upon time set by the action plan. The participants in the restorative circle had agreed to take certain actions that they believed would bring about healing, harmony, or ease; help make amends; and provide occasions for mutual support. And in the postcircle, they gather to assess their level of satisfaction with the actions taken. Every person has an opportunity to acknowledge the contributions of the others and to express gratitude. At the same time, each person assesses whether anything further is needed to bring about the agreed-upon aims of the circle. What further actions might be taken that would contribute to the healing, peace, or reconciliation of the community?

Perhaps the actions they took did not meet their needs in the ways they had anticipated. Now they can propose new actions based on newly discovered needs. When the group explores the meaning of these actions for each participant, community connections are further deepened. Each participant has an opportunity to delve more deeply into the meaning the proposed actions carry for her personally, as she is now newly aware of them. Can something further be done to capture the essence of what is at stake? Have new circumstances arisen that now need to be considered?

If the agreed-upon actions were not in fact carried out, the postcircle offers an opportunity to explore what needs were met by *not* following through on those actions. That is to say, what are the reasons for anyone choosing not to follow through on the action plan? What needs would not have been met by undertaking the action? The postcircle provides an opportunity to fine-tune the action plan, in other words, not to blame or shame those who did not follow through on the agreement. Newly discovered needs may then lead to a new action plan within a new time frame.[38]

As before, the facilitator will check with each speaker whether he has been heard to his own satisfaction by asking another to repeat the essence of what is important to the one who just spoke. This step continues to be crucial because it closes the communication loop. Trust in the process is deepened as people discover that what matters to them has been fully heard.

Churches not in the midst of crises would be wise to consider the principles of restorative practice and agree to create a restorative system in which to nest any particular restorative circle. A church doesn't have to be in the midst of conflict to become a restorative congregation. Indeed, proactive circles that are not responding to crisis can be established to deepen relational ties. Circles can be developed as the church's normal way of doing business. For example, a church council meeting could be conducted, not according to Robert's Rules of Order, but rather according to a circle process. Youth groups might agree to check in with each other (with a talking piece) by describing the highs and lows of their week. An upcoming issue that is not contentious could be discussed in church-wide circle processes. By these means the church would model in all their practices that everyone's voice matters; that processes are invitational, not coerced; and that those in power positions are not seeking to assert power over others but want to empower all members to participate in the crucial decisions of the community. Decisions will still be made by those responsible to make them (e.g., staff, council, pastors, etc.), but members will grow in trust that their voices will be heard about issues that matter to them. Restorative circles are inscribed as a way of life for the community.

When institutional agreements are in place for how conflicts are to be approached, a community is more readily prepared to use any given conflict as an opportunity for growth. Physical space needs to be set aside

38. The aims and procedures of both pre- and postcircles represent my understanding of Dominic Barter's teachings as presented in his workshop "Building Compassionate Justice for 21st Century."

where circles can be conducted. Members of the community need to be trained to facilitate circles at the lower end of conflict intensity. The process for requesting a restorative circle needs to be made accessible to all members, so that all persons are equally empowered.[39]

Conclusion

The purpose of this chapter has been to introduce the field of restorative practices to the contemporary church as a way to promote mutual understanding, self-responsibility, and effective action in communities torn apart by conflict or shocked by trauma. While restorative processes are deeply embedded in the theology and history of the church — especially in the so-called historic "peace" communions — they are rarely given the place they deserve, at least in mainline denominations in the United States. Yet, because forgiveness and reconciliation lie at the core of the gospel, the church, for the sake of its basic integrity, needs to be tireless in aligning its relational practices with its beliefs.

In his book *The Tacit Dimension,* Michael Polanyi writes:

> To rely on a theory for understanding nature is to interiorize it. For we are attending from the theory to things seen in its light, and we are aware of the theory, while thus using it, in terms of the spectacle that it serves to explain. This is why mathematical theory can be learned only by practicing its application: its true knowledge lies in our ability to use it. . . . A true knowledge of a theory can be established only after it has been interiorized and extensively used to interpret experience.[40]

Conceptual models, such as the one presented here, become tools for knowing only when we indwell both the model and the situation at hand. Does the model illuminate the situation? How? Does it fail to account for certain factors? In what way? Does it open up new avenues for further investigation?

---

39. The importance of creating a community-wide agreement to a restorative system is a major point of emphasis in Barter's teaching. Without this institutional understanding and agreement in place, any restorative circle would have little impact on the congregational culture as a whole.

40. Michael Polanyi, *The Tacit Dimension* (Garden City, N.Y.: Anchor Books, 1967), 17-21.

I believe that restorative practices have a great deal to offer churches that are struggling with entrenched conflict or reeling from traumatic events in their lives. The model also offers clear and simple guidelines for reaching across any of the normal barriers that separate human beings in community. When differences become barriers to understanding, restorative circles have much to commend them. Whether the differences are racial, cultural, political, or religious does not seem to matter. Circles such as those described here will facilitate mutual understanding, self-responsibility, and new creative action. That is perhaps why they are used increasingly in a wide variety of venues: in education, criminal justice, and social service agencies. Once the basic principles and practices are understood, circles can be adopted in an even wider variety of contexts. Individual families might use these simple guidelines to deepen relational ties among their members.[41] Those trained in facilitation in their churches will be able to use these uncomplicated skills wherever they go; these skills will contribute substantively to any community of which they are a part.

Churches that decide to adopt restorative practices for their communities provide opportunities for their members to learn more honest and caring ways to communicate. They give visible shape to the church's commitment to speak the truth in love, not as an abstract ideal to strive for but as a growing skill that will empower the community to take responsibility for its own conflicts. Working through interpersonal pain is one way of trusting in God's grace. In honoring the interdependent needs of every member, in facilitating mutual understanding, and in offering opportunities for real accountability, the gospel of Jesus Christ can be lived out.

These practices have the potential to develop each member's capacity to see the human beings with whom she is in conflict as precious members of the body of Christ, brothers and sisters made in the image of God, not as opponents to be controlled or conquered. The circle process enables each person to participate as a fully equal and valued member of the community. All members are given an opportunity to cocreate constructive solutions. In the process, every member who participates will learn crucial skills in how to undertake dialogue in a respectful way.

Every voice is valued as the whole body together seeks God's kingdom. "Again, truly I tell you, if two of you agree on earth about anything you ask, it will be done for you by my Father in heaven. For where two or three are

41. Kay Pranis, *The Little Book of Circle Processes* (Intercourse, Pa.: Good Books, 2005), 65-66.

gathered in my name, I am there among them" (Matt. 18:19-20 NRSV). The fundamental interdependence of the members of the body is essential to this understanding. Emphasis is squarely placed on the unity of the body of Christ, even though each member plays a unique, indispensable role. We are members of one another, and "if one member suffers, all suffer together with it" (1 Cor. 12:26 NRSV). Jesus reminds his disciples over and over again that even "the least of these" matter in the kingdom of God. Restorative circles offer a structure in which the members of the church can experience the truth that everyone does in fact matter.

Restorative circles highlight the fact that all our choices are made in the context of mutual accountability. As we listen to one another, we gain a wider vision of how our words and actions have affected others in the community. If we regret our choices, we are given an opportunity to make amends. Since all members are treated with basic respect, acknowledging regret does not humiliate a person. On the contrary, it is a sign of the Holy Spirit's work in our midst. As churches offer safe places to strengthen frayed bonds of trust, and as they call upon God to minister to the community in its pain, they give opportunities for each person to express what has wounded the person most. Restorative circles offer a safe structure, a clear process, and a healing intention for members of the body to hear one another's stories in a public forum. Now the hurting parties can be heard respectfully. It takes time to heal. Even more importantly, it takes willingness. No one can make another willing to begin such a healing journey, but without clear processes in place, no healing journey can ever be begun. Such circles offer the church concrete practices for working through churchwide impasses where mutual understanding, genuine accountability, and basic trust are the core needs of the community. Out of such honestly faced conflict, new life and hope will, by the grace of God, spring up.

Criteria for PTSD

Diagnostic and Statistical Manual–5

The American Psychiatric Association's latest edition of the Diagnostic and Statistical Manual (DSM-5), released in 2014, specifies eight criteria for diagnosing PTSD. Of course, ministers and pastoral caregivers are not responsible for making medical diagnoses. Nevertheless, someone suffering from a traumatic response to stress can understand a great deal by becoming familiar with these criteria.

1. The person is exposed to death, threatened death, or serious injury or sexual violence (or is a witness of such).
2. The person experiences recurrent, involuntary, and intrusive memories, nightmares, or flashbacks.
3. The person tries to avoid trauma-related thoughts or feelings or possible external reminders of the trauma.
4. The person has negative alterations in thought and mood, that is, two of the following symptoms: persistent and distorted negative beliefs and expectations about oneself or the world; persistent emotions such as fear, horror, anger, guilt, or shame; a sense of alienation from others; or diminished interest in (pretraumatic) significant activities.
5. The person experiences trauma-related reactivity (two required: hypervigilance, aggressive or reckless behavior, startle response, sleep disturbances).
6. The symptoms persist for more than a month.
7. The symptoms cause significant distress or functional impairment.
8. These disturbances are not due to medication, illness, or the use of substances.

Two other provisos are mentioned:

1. Sometimes dissociative symptoms (depersonalization and derealization) are present and sometimes not. *Depersonalization:* experience of being an outside observer of or being detached from oneself (e.g., feeling as if "this is not happening to me" or one were in a dream). *Derealization:* experience of unreality, distance, or distortion (e.g., "things are not real").
2. Sometimes the full diagnosis is not warranted until at least six months after the event, although the onset of some symptoms may occur immediately.

This page is an abbreviated synopsis of the information found at http://www.ptsd.va.gov/professional/pages/dsm5_criteria_ptsd.asp, accessed August 1, 2013.

Professional Quality of Life Scale

Compassion Satisfaction and Fatigue Subscales — Revision IV

[Helping] people puts you in direct contact with their lives. As you probably have experienced, your compassion for those you [help] has both positive and negative aspects. We would like to ask you questions about your experiences, both positive and negative, as a [helper]. Consider each of the following questions about you and your current situation. Select the number that honestly reflects how frequently you experienced these characteristics in the last 30 days.

0 = Never
1 = Rarely
2 = A Few Times
3 = Somewhat Often
4 = Often
5 = Very Often

1. I am happy.
2. I am preoccupied with more than one person I [*help*].
3. I get satisfaction from being able to [*help*] people.
4. I feel connected to others.
5. I jump or am startled by unexpected sounds.
6. I feel invigorated after working with those I [*help*].
7. I find it difficult to separate my personal life from my *life* as a [*helper*].
8. I am losing sleep over traumatic experiences of a person I [*help*].
9. I think that I might have been "infected" by the traumatic stress of those I [*help*].

10. I feel trapped by my work as a [*helper*].
11. Because of my [*helping*], I have felt "on edge" about various things.
12. I like my work as a [*helper*].
13. I feel depressed as a result of my work as a [*helper*].
14. I feel as though I am experiencing the trauma of someone I have [*helped*].
15. I have beliefs that sustain me.
16. I am pleased with how I am able to keep up with [*helping*] techniques and protocols.
17. I am the person I always wanted to be.
18. My work makes me feel satisfied.
19. Because of my work as a [*helper*], I feel exhausted.
20. I have happy thoughts and feelings about those I [*help*] and how I could help them.
21. I feel overwhelmed by the amount of work or the size of my *case[work] load* I have to deal with.
22. I believe I can make a difference through my work.
23. I avoid certain activities or situations because they remind me of frightening experiences of the people I [*help*].
24. I am proud of what I can do to [*help*].
25. As a result of my [*helping*], I have intrusive, frightening thoughts.
26. I feel "bogged down" by the system.
27. I have thoughts that I am a "success" as a [*helper*].
28. I can't recall important parts of my work with trauma victims.
29. I am a very sensitive person.
30. I am happy that I chose to do this work.

You may substitute the appropriate target group for *[helper]* if that is not the best term. For example, if you are working with teachers, replace *[helper]* with "teacher." Word changes may be made to any word in italicized square brackets to make the measure read more smoothly for a particular target group.

Self-Scoring Directions, If Used as a Self-Test

1. Be certain you respond to all items.
2. On some items the scores need to be reversed. Next to your response write the reverse of that score (i.e., 0 = 0, 1 = 5, 2 = 4, 3 = 3). Reverse

the scores on these 5 items: 1, 4, 15, 17 and 29. Please note that the value 0 is not reversed, as its value is always null.

3. Mark the items for scoring:
   a. Put an X by the 10 items that form the Compassion Satisfaction Scale: 3, 6, 12, 16, 18, 20, 22, 24, 27, 30.
   b. Put a check by the 10 items on the Burnout Scale: 1, 4, 8, 10, 15, 17, 19, 21, 26, 29.
   c. Circle the 10 items on the Trauma/Compassion Fatigue Scale: 2, 5, 7, 9, 11, 13, 14, 23, 25, 28.
4. Add the numbers you wrote next to the items for each set of items and compare with the theoretical scores.

Your Scores on the ProQOL: Professional Quality of Life Screening

Based on your responses, your personal scores are below. If you have any concerns, you should discuss them with a physical or mental health care professional.

Compassion Satisfaction _____

Compassion satisfaction is about the pleasure you derive from being able to do your work well. For example, you may feel like it is a pleasure to help others through your work. You may feel positively about your colleagues or your ability to contribute to the work setting or even the greater good of society. Higher scores on this scale represent a greater satisfaction related to your ability to be an effective caregiver in your job.

The average score is 37 (SO 7; alpha scale reliability .87). About 25% of people score higher than 42 and about 25% of people score below 33. If you are in the higher range, you probably derive a good deal of professional satisfaction from your position. If your scores are below 33, you may either find problems with your job, or there may be some other reason — for example, you might derive your satisfaction from activities other than your job.

Burnout _____

Most people have an intuitive idea of what burnout is. From the research perspective, burnout is associated with feelings of hopelessness and difficulties in dealing with work or in doing your job effectively. These negative feelings usually have a gradual onset. They can reflect the feeling that your *efforts* make no difference, or they can be associated with a very high workload or a non-supportive work environment. Higher scores on this scale mean that you are at higher risk for burnout.

The average score on the burnout scale is 22 (SO 6.0; alpha scale reliability .72). About 25% of people score above 27 and about 25% of people score below 18. If your score is below 18, this probably reflects positive feelings about your ability to be effective in your work. If you score above 27 you may wish to think about what at work makes you feel like you are not effective in your position. Your score may reflect your mood; perhaps you were having a "bad day" or are in need of some time off. If the high score persists or if it is reflective of other worries, it may be a cause for concern.

Compassion Fatigue/Secondary Trauma _____

Compassion fatigue (CF), also called secondary trauma (STS) and related to Vicarious Trauma (VT), is about your work-related, secondary exposure to extremely stressful events. For example, you may repeatedly hear stories about the traumatic things that happen to other people, commonly called VT. If your work puts you directly in the path of danger, such as being a soldier or humanitarian aid worker, this is not secondary exposure; your exposure is primary. However, if you are exposed to others' traumatic events as a result of your work, such as in an emergency room or working with child protective services, this is secondary exposure. The symptoms of CF/STS are usually rapid in onset and associated with a particular event. They may include being afraid, having difficulty sleeping, having images of the upsetting event pop into your mind, or avoiding things that remind you of the event.

The average score on this scale is 13 (SO 6; alpha scale reliability .80). About 25% of people score below 8 and about 25% of people score above 17. If your score is above 17, you may want to take some time to think about what at work may be frightening to you or if there is some other reason for the elevated score. While higher scores do not mean that you do have a problem, they are an indication that you may want to examine how you feel about your work and your work environment. You may wish to discuss this with your supervisor, a colleague, or a health care professional.

Disclaimer: This information is presented for educational purposes only.

It is not a substitute for informed medical advice or training. Do not use this information to diagnose or treat a health problem without consulting a qualified health or mental health care provider. If you have concerns, contact your health care provider, mental health professional, or your community health center.

For more information on the ProQOL, go to
http://www.isu.edu/~bhstamm

Index

Index

Taboo, 50, 57, 130

Tall, Deborah, 97

Tedeshi, R. G., 40

Telos, xiv, 14, 121, 129

Terrorism, xi

Theology, ix, xii, xiii, xiv, 1, 2, 14, 22, 40, 64, 65, 78, 86, 102, 112, 118, 119, 124, 129, 130, 146

Therapist, xiii, 15, 16, 23, 29, 33-35, 39, 50, 59, 62, 68, 119, 120

Therapy, 4, 42, 47, 59, 60, 63, 67, 105

Torture, xi, 1, 2, 22, 71-74, 77, 79, 81, 90

Transdisciplinary studies, ix, 124

Transgender, 28

Trauma, traumatic, vii, ix, xi, xii, xiv, xv, 1-16, 18-25, 28-31, 35, 39-41, 46, 48, 58, 61, 63, 68, 70, 72, 98, 116, 122-24, 136, 142, 146, 147, 149, 151, 152, 154
  intergenerational trauma, xi
  interpersonal trauma, xi
  secondary traumatic stress, 29, 30
  traumatic event, 4, 6, 7, 19, 46, 147, 154
  traumatic loss, 1, 2
  traumatic response, 149
  vicarious traumatic stress, xiv, 28, 29

Treatment, xii, 6, 12, 24, 66, 72

Trible, Phyllis, 2

Trust, xi, xiii, 2, 11-14, 16, 19, 20, 26, 31-33, 36-38, 41, 43-45, 56, 59, 62, 67, 73, 75, 76, 79, 80, 84, 86, 88, 89, 103, 105, 109, 117, 132-35, 142, 144, 145, 147, 148

Truth and Reconciliation Commission, 15, 124

Tsuris, 39

Tutsis, 103, 110

Tutu, Desmond, 15, 16, 34, 35, 124, 129

Ubuntu, 34, 35, 129

Ulanov, Ann Belford, ix, 9, 10, 15

Unconscious, unconsciously, 9, 52, 53, 54, 56, 58, 59

Vennen, Mark Vander, ix, 125

Veterans, 3, 10, 71, 72

Vicarious trauma, 116, 154

Vicarious traumatic stress, xiv, 28, 29

Victim, xv, 6, 8, 9, 14, 16, 19, 22, 23, 28, 32, 33, 43, 45, 57-59, 65, 67, 72, 131, 139, 140, 152

Vietnam, 3, 10, 71

Violence, xi, 2, 4, 9, 10, 19, 22-24, 26, 28, 30, 43, 45, 63, 65-67, 70, 92, 103, 116, 149
  domestic violence, xi, 2, 3
  structural violence, 9, 28, 29, 35

Vitek, W., 97

Volkan, Vamik, 19

Vulnerable, 4, 13, 19, 23, 28, 35, 82, 83, 85, 95, 118, 121, 131

Wachtel, Ted, 125, 126

War, ix, 2, 3, 10, 22, 35, 43, 54, 61, 71, 72

Webster, John, 78, 118

Weibe, Katherine, 19, 21

Weingarten, Kaethe, xiii, 4, 18, 22-41

Weisaeth, Lars, 4, 5, 7, 12

Well-being, 29, 103, 126, 130, 139

Wheeler, Barbara G., 36, 127

Whyte, David, 98, 99

Wilde, Oscar, 95, 96

Wilmer, Harry A., 10, 71, 72

Wisdom, xii, 11, 13, 27, 35, 66, 80, 114, 131

Witness/witnessing, vii, xiii-xv, 2, 4, 12, 13, 18, 22-36, 38, 40, 41, 82, 92, 93, 98, 102, 103, 112, 134, 149
  compassionate witness, vii, 21, 22, 23, 26, 28, 29, 30, 36, 40
  empowered/disempowered witness, xiii, 31
  loving witness, 18

Wolterstorff, Nicholas, 41, 90, 91, 99

Workaholism, 8

Worship, 2, 20, 21, 68, 79, 81, 90, 103, 116

Yehuda, Rachel, 5

Yiddish, 39

Yoder, Carolyn, 5, 8

Zehr, Howard, 9, 14, 19, 20, 23, 124, 136